EVERYMAN'S
BOOK OF
CHILDREN'S GAMES
GYLES
BRANDRETH

For my mother
Alice Brandreth
and three of her grandchildren:
Benet, Saethryd and Aphra Brandreth

EVERYMAN'S
BOOK OF
CHILDREN'S
GAMES

GYLES
BRANDRETH

J. M. Dent & Sons Ltd
London Melbourne

First published 1984
First published in paperback, 1985
© Gyles Brandreth 1984

This book is set in VIP Melior by
D. P. Media Limited, Hitchin, Hertfordshire

Printed in Great Britain by
Guernsey Press Co. Ltd, Guernsey C.I., for
J. M. Dent & Sons Ltd
Aldine House, 33 Welbeck Street, London W1M 8LX

British Library Cataloguing in Publication Data

Brandreth, Gyles
    Everyman's book of children's games.
    1. Games—Juvenile literature
    I. Title
    790.1'922   GV1203

    ISBN 0-460-02426-4

CONTENTS

Introduction xi

GAMES TO PLAY AT HOME

Games for the Very Young
The Alphabet Race 2
Socky Ball 2
Hot Boiled Beans and Bacon 3
Birds Fly 3
Sing a Song of Sixpence 4
Penny Dropping 5
The Farmer's in His Den 5
A-Hunting We Will Go 6
Zoo Twins 7
Pat-a-Cake 7
Three Blind Mice 8
Daylight Robbery 9
Busy Bees 9
Here We Come Gathering Nuts in May 10
Choo-Choo Tag 11

Quick and Easy
Flap Ears 11
Fizz-Buzz 12
Who Leads? 12
Lemon Relay 13
Break Out 13
Rattle Catcher 14
Card Targets 14
King of the Castle 14

Gora 15
Giant's Steps 15
Up and Over Down and Under 16
Jousting 16
Stretch and Bend 16
Fire! Fire! 17
Dragon Heads and Tails 17
Roundabout Escape 18
Balloon Buffeting 18

Word Games
Coffee Pot 19
Word Chains 19
Minute Words 20
A Was an Apple Pie 20
Famous Fives 21
I Love My Love 21
Tourist Trail 22
Consonant Catalogue 22
Animal, Vegetable, or Mineral 23
Who Am I? 23
Spelling Bee 24
Capital Catching 24
Sentences 24
Traveller's Tales 25
Rhyme Counting 26
Tennis, Elbow, Foot 26

Word Wise 27
Snip 27
ZYX 28

Paper and Pencil Games
Hangman 28
Battleships 29
Boxes 30
News Line 31
Mirror Images 31
Join the Numbers 32
Guess in the Dark 32
First Names First 33
Squaring Up 33
The Worm 34
Picture Consequences 35
Smell It Out 35
Pairing Up 36

Card Games
Pelmanism 36
Snap 37
Old Maid 38
Snip-Snap-Snorem 39
Happy Families 39
Donkey 40
Cheat 41
Rolling Stone 42
Round the Corner 42
My Ship Sails 43
Go Boom 44
Beggar My Neighbour 44
War 45
Rummy 46

Board Games
Nine Men's Morris 47
Achi 48
Nine Holes 49
Four Field Kono 49
Gobang 50
Chess 51
Horseshoe 55
Grasshopper 55
Madelinette 56
Draughts 57
Mu-Torere 58
Reversi 59
Alquerque 60
Fox and Geese 61

Games with Bits and Pieces
Spangy 62
Bounce Eye 63
Ring Taw 63
Dice Shot 64
Beetle 64
Hearts 66
Pig 66
Round the Clock 67
Chicago 68
Fifty 68
Kayles 69
Nim 69
Ends 70
Fours 70
Blocking 71
Blind Hughie 71

GAMES TO PLAY AT SCHOOL

Playgroup Games
Traffic Lights 74

Hide and Seek 74
Button Bag 75

Bingo 75
Across the Great Divide 76
Name Chain 76
Teacher 77
Colour Dip 77
Shopping 78
Spot the Number 78
Obstacle Courses 79
Mind Reading 79
Follow My Leader 80
Alphabet Angling 80

Classroom Games
Draughts-Board Observation 81
Buried Words 81
Synonyms 82
Colour Changes 82
Ship Game 83
Heights 83
Conversations 84
What's Changed 84
The Dog and the Cat 84
Book Spotting 85
Round-the-World Relay 86
Just a Minute 87
Hunt the Alphabet 87
Scrambles 87

Playground Games
King Caesar 88
American Hopscotch 88
Snail, or French Hop 90
Touch Wood and Whistle 90
Jack, Jack, the Bread Burns 91
The Huntsman and the Hares 91
Sevens 92
North, South, East and West 92
Ball Trap 93
The White Spot 93
Tag 93
Hopping Home 94

Playing-Field Games
Foodor 95
Whoop 95
Balloon Tennis 96
Crab Scuttle Relay 96
Whack and Catch 96
Kangaroo Racing 97
Handkerchief 97
Pall Mall 98
Rounders 98
Hop, Step and Jump 99
Clear the Mark Leap-Frog 100
Square Chasing 100
Jolly Miller 101

PARTY GAMES

Planning a Children's Party
Planning Tips 105
Food and Drink 106
The Party Itself – What to do 106

Parlour Games
Fish Pond 107
Initial I-Spy 108

The Floating Feather 108
Cat and Mouse 109
Squeak, Piggy, Squeak 109
Pennies in the Circle 110
Farmyard 110
Hop Rabbit Hop! 111
Blind Man's Buff 111
Hunt the Thimble 112

Grandmother's Footsteps 113
Blind Man's Treasure Hunt 113
The Donkey's Tail 114
Winking 115
Spinning the Plate 115

Musical Games
Musical Arches 116
Paul Jones 116
Musical Hotch-Potch 117
Musical Bumps 117
Oranges and Lemons 118
Musical Islands 119
Musical Reflexes 119
Musical Chairs 120
Musical Walking Stick 120
Musical Statues 121
The Grand Old Duke of York 121
Here We Go Round the Mulberry
  Bush 122
Musical Posture 123
Grand Chain 123
London Bridge 124
Musical Slipper 124
Musical Numbers 125
Musical Hats 125

Racing Games
Waiter! Waiter! 126
Thimble Race 126
Back to Front Race 127
Potato Race 127
Drop the Lot 128
Balloon Sweeping 128
Marbles Race 129
Ankle Race 129
Pick and Cup Race 130
Snail's Race 130
Feather Race 131
Fish Pool 131
Doll Dressing Race 132

Burst the Bag Race 132
Dressing-up Race 133

Talking Games
I Packed My Bag 134
Secrets 134
The Judge 135
Backward Spelling 135
What Are We Shouting? 135
Poison Letters 136
Donkey 137
The Old Oak Chest 138
I Spy 138
The Minister's Cat 139
Don't Stop Talking 139
Twenty Questions 140
What's My Name 140
Sausages 141
I Want a Rhyme 141

Acting Games
Charades 142
Act the Word 143
Dumb Show 144
Dumb Crambo 144
Simon Says 145
Dumb Nursery Rhymes 145
Noah's Ark 146
Acting Clumps 147
What Are We? 147
Destination Please? 148
Poor Pussy 148
Acting Proverbs 149
Please Pass 150

Paper and Pencil Games
Kim's Game 150
Dotty Drawings 151
Jumbled Proverbs 152
Heads and Tails 152
Sounds Off 153

Constantinople 153
Find the Adjectives 154
Word Power 154
Ten Pennies 155
Consequences 155
Letter Sentence 156
Picture Spotting 156
Blindfold Drawing 157
Feel It 158
Missing Vowels 158

Home Entertainment
Hand Puppets 159
Magic Discs 160
Lifting the Ice Cube 161
Age Telling 161
Tongue Twisters 163
Disappearing Coin 164
The Game of Shadows 164
Shadow Shows 165

ALLSORTS

Games for Journeys
Hic, Haec, Hoc 168
Mora 169
Shoot 169
Number-Plate Numbers 170
Alphabetical Sentences 170
Geography 171
Number-Plate Messages 171
Sir Tommy 172
Spoof 173
Mile's End 173
Word Watching 174
Build Up 174
Observation 175
A to Z 176
Fish 176
Colour Contest 177

Games for Holidays
Islands 177
Queenie 178
Corko 178
The Boiler Burst 179
Pavement Bullboard 179
Crossing Out Letters 180
Slap Jack 181

Snow Snake 101
Triangular Tug of War 182
Newspaper Quiz 182
Squat Tag 182
Touch Tag 183
Eh, Bee, Sea 183

Seaside Games
Beach Golf 184
Pin Weed 185
Hopscotch 185
Water Relay 186
Middle Man 187
French Cricket 187
Twigs 188
King Canute's Game 188
Beach Olympics 189
Three Against One 190
Skimmers 190
The Shebble Game 191
Catch and Pull 191
Squirts 192

Seasonal Games
Romeo and Juliet 192
Heart Throbs 193

Hole in the Sheet *193*
Egg Guessing *194*
Easter Bunnies and Chicks *194*
Easter Egg Relay *195*
Musical Torch *195*
Apple Ducking *196*
Jingle Bells *196*
Merry Christmas *197*
Christmas Stocking Story *197*
Christmas Card Hunt *198*

Sickbed Games
Concentration *198*
The Nation Game *199*
Word Links *199*
The Unicorn Game *199*
My House *200*
Pyramids *200*
Where Am I? *201*
The Shortest Word *202*
Name Messages *203*
Clock Cards *203*
Siege *204*
Bright or Cloudy *205*

INTRODUCTION

It was the British Prime Minister David Lloyd George who, in 1925, made a forthright and significant assertion: 'The right to play is a child's first claim on the community. No community can infringe that right without doing deep and enduring harm to the minds and bodies of its citizens.' He was right. Playing games is a vital part of every child's development and that is why I have done my best to make sure that this book is useful as well as entertaining.

Of course, play is not peculiar to the human species. It can be observed throughout the animal kingdom as an instructive activity through which the young prepare for adult life. Because games of all kinds become an instinctive preparation for adulthood, the way our children play their games and the circumstances in which they play tell us something about the future of our society. And because it is an instinctive need – as well, incidentally, as a human right recognized formally by the United Nations' Declaration of the Rights of Children – children will play, irrespective of what we provide for them in terms of ideas and opportunities.

For some inexplicable reason, many adults treat games-playing as something trivial and unimportant. At best it keeps the kids out of mischief and provides an alternative to watching television; at worst it is considered a frivolous waste of time, enjoyable for the child perhaps, but of no specific value. In fact, for children play is not the opposite of work: it is both a vital element in their healthy and happy development and a crucial form of communication with adults, especially their parents.

We need to encourage our children to play by themselves and we need to be ready and willing to play with them ourselves. Recent studies (at Groningen University in the Netherlands) have established beyond question that a lack of adult involvement leads to a reduction in the capacity for children to play imaginatively and creatively. At a recent International Play Conference a speaker from Cornell University in the United States produced evidence suggesting that all industrialized societies are facing the problem of decreasing motivation and performance among school children. One factor, he said, was the deteriorating environment for children; another, the decreasing involvement of adults with children.

I am placing such emphasis on the need for adult involvement in children's games partly because, through becoming involved in the work of the National Playing Fields Association in Britain, I have realized how tremendously important it is, and partly because I want you to have the pleasure of discovering that if you regularly play games with your children not only will they have more fun, but you will too.

All the games described in this book are ones that can be enjoyed by adults as well as children. Some of them definitely require an adult to organize and oversee; others, probably the majority, are games where adults can play with children as fellow players rather than as official supervisors. I have tried to make the collection as comprehensive and eclectic as space allowed, and have done my best to provide all the standard games you would expect to find in an encyclopaedia of children's games as well as a good number of surprises.

The book opens with sections of Games to Play at Home and Games to Play at School, but the divisions are not to be adhered to strictly: it doesn't matter if you play Donkey at home or at school, in a playgroup or on a playing field. Similarly, while the section devoted to Party Games opens with a few thoughts on planning and giving a children's party, I believe Blind Man's Buff is far too good a game to play just at parties. The last section is called Allsorts and contains those games that are geared to specific times and places: games for journeys and for holidays, games to play beside the sea, games with special seasonal associations, and games that work well with children who are unwell and in bed or simply listless. At the beginning of the description of each game, as well as listing the details of any equipment or supervision that may be required, I have given a rough indication of the age range to which the particular game seems most to appeal, plus an estimate of the minimum length of time needed to play just one round of the game in question. I have also indicated (by means of an * against the title) whether or not a game has a competitive element in it, as I have found that many of the most enjoyable – and stimulating and rewarding – games are the ones that nobody 'wins'. Sometimes, for general interest, I have included a few details on the origin of a game.

Many of the games in the book are ones I have been playing all my life. A good number I have discovered as a parent myself, as a teacher in schools in Britain and America, and as a children's author meeting young people from the age of three upwards in playgroups and schools and libraries. I was introduced to several of the most interesting and exciting games by my colleagues at the National Playing Fields Association, and I would like particularly to acknowledge my debt to Peter Heseltine, John Holborn and Josephine Seccombe.

When I started to compile this book I already knew that play was important. By the time I had finished I had learnt that it was fun as well. When you have worked your way through from *The Alphabet Race* (page 2) to *Bright or Cloudy* (page 205), via *Fizz Buzz* and *Coffee Pot* and *Smell It Out* and *Cheat* and *Grasshopper* and *Pig* and *Twigs* and scores more, I hope you will agree.

Gyles Brandreth

GAMES TO PLAY AT HOME

Games for the Very Young
Quick and Easy
Word Games
Paper and Pencil Games
Card Games
Board Games
Games with Bits and Pieces

GAMES FOR THE VERY YOUNG

The Alphabet Race *

Number: any number   *Age:* 3–5   *Time:* 2–3 minutes
Adult supervision: checking completed alphabets
(*Equipment:* a set of alphabet cards per child)

Each set of alphabet cards consists of twenty-six cards, each bearing a letter of the alphabet. These are given to the children (one set per child) all jumbled up with the letters totally out of sequence. On the word 'Go' the children have to arrange the cards in the correct order. The first to do this is the winner.

Socky Ball (* if the children like competition)

Number: any number   *Age:* 3–6   *Time:* 5–10 minutes (longer if they're happy)   *Adult supervision:* keeping score and giving encouragement   (*Equipment:* a pair of socks and a pair of adult's shoes)

Children playing with balls inside the house can cause problems. Objects can get knocked over, windows have been known to break and there is always the risk that the ball might be left for some hapless adult to tread on and twist an ankle, or worse. Children love playing with balls all the same, and given a chance to throw one few children will refuse. If the balls are so soft that they can't cause any damage, then everyone's happy, and by using a pair of socks to make the ball you reach the perfect solution.

All you do is roll up the socks and tuck the top of one over them both to form a soft ball. Set up a pair of adult shoes as a target and let the children aim their throws at those. Nothing can be broken and they can't damage the paintwork or wallpaper. The shoes should be placed against a wall with the toes pointing towards the thrower. Raise the heels by placing a couple of books underneath them to make landing the sock ball inside a little easier.

You can either keep a score of the number of successful throws out of ten, say, or you can let the children take it in turns and just enjoy improving their skill.

Hot Boiled Beans and Bacon

Number: any number   *Age:* 4–6   *Time:* 5–10 minutes   *Adult supervision:* hiding objects to be found by players   (*Equipment:* something small to be hidden – a little toy or a walnut, for example)

This is a North American version of the well-known searching game *Hot and Cold* adored by children all over the world.

One of the players leaves the room and the small article is hidden in full view of the others. When everyone is ready the children in the room chant: 'Hot boiled beans and bacon; now it's hidden and can be taken!' Hearing this the player outside the room enters and starts searching for the hidden object. If he gets near the hiding place, the others can shout 'Hot'; and if the player gets very near they can shout 'Burning'. But a player who moves away from the hidden object will only receive shouts of 'Cold'. Guided in this way the player will soon find whatever has been hidden, giving someone else the chance to go outside the door while the object is hidden again for the next round.

Birds Fly *

Number: any number   *Age:* 3–6   *Time:* 3–5 minutes
Adult supervision: acting as the leader

Sit all the players on the floor with both hands on the ground. Their hands must stay on the ground unless the leader mentions a creature that flies, in which case they must raise both hands in the air.

The leader might say 'Eagles fly', and all the arms would shoot into the air. He or she might say 'Pigeons fly', and the same would happen. But if the leader says 'Elephants fly', any arms that are raised knock their owner out of the game. The last one left in is the winner.

After the first game let the children take it in turns to be leader. You'll find that their knowledge of flying creatures builds up surprisingly quickly, but keep an ear open for any creatures taking to the skies in error; the cow may jump over the moon in the nursery rhyme, but it's as well to correct the idea about the real ones that provide our milk!

Sing a Song of Sixpence

Number: any number   *Age:* 3–5   *Time:* 1 minute   *Adult supervision:* leading the singing (if necessary)

If everyone knows the words of the nursery rhyme, all you have to tell them is that they should act out the movements as they sing the words (you can lead them in this). If they don't know the words, it doesn't matter. Just sing the nursery rhyme yourself and get them to follow your movements. They may want to try it themselves after going through it once with your help.

Stand all the players in front of you so that they can see what you are doing, and start singing:

> Sing a song of sixpence
> A pocket full of rye,
> (Hands in pockets)
>
> Four and twenty blackbirds
> (Fly like blackbirds with flapping arms)
>
> Baked in a pie,
> (Noses smelling delicious pie)
>
> When the pie was opened
> The birds began to sing,
> (Mouthing singing)
>
> Wasn't that a dainty dish
> To set before the king?
> (Offering dish to king)
>
> The king was in his counting house,
> Counting out his money,
> (Counting money from a bag)
>
> The queen was in the parlour
> Eating bread and honey,
> (Miming eating)
>
> The maid was in the garden
> Hanging up the clothes,
> (Miming hanging up clothes)
>
> When down came a blackbird
> And pecked off her nose!
> (All the players tweak their noses!)

Penny Dropping *

Number: any number   *Age:* 4–6   *Time:* 10 minutes or more
Adult supervision: checking on accuracy of players
(*Equipment:* a bucket of water, 1 five-pence coin and 6 two-pence coins per player)

Children will play happily at this simple game for ten minutes or more once they get the hang of it – particularly if they can win 5p!

Place the coin in the bottom of the bucket and cover it with about 15 centimetres (6 inches) of water. Give each of the children six 2p coins (or get them to share the six coins), and let them drop the coins into the bucket with the idea of landing one on the 5p and covering it. The first player to do this wins the 5p, but have a few more available so that others can win one too.

The Farmer's in His Den

Number: any number   *Age:* 4–6   *Time:* 1–2 minutes per round
Adult supervision: leading the singing (if necessary)

One player becomes the farmer and stands in the middle of a circle formed by the others joining hands. The circle walks round singing:

> The farmer's in his den
> The farmer's in his den
> Heigh-ho heigh-ho
> The farmer's in his den.
>
> The farmer wants a wife
> The farmer wants a wife
> Heigh-ho heigh ho
> The farmer wants a wife.

At the end of the verse the circle stops and the farmer chooses one player to be his wife, who joins him in the middle. The circle joins hands again for the second verse which is sung as it walks round:

> The wife wants a child
> The wife wants a child
> Heigh-ho heigh-ho
> The wife wants a child.

When the circle stops this time it's the wife's turn to choose a player. She wants a child and picks one of the players to join her and the farmer in the middle. The circle joins hands and sets off for the next verse:

> The child wants a nurse
> The child wants a nurse
> Heigh-ho heigh-ho
> The child wants a nurse.

The child picks a nurse from the circle which walks round once more to sing:

> The nurse wants a dog
> The nurse wants a dog
> Heigh-ho heigh-ho
> The nurse wants a dog.

The nurse chooses a dog and they all sing the last verse:

> We all pat the dog
> We all pat the dog
> Heigh-ho heigh-ho
> We all pat the dog.

Everyone pats the dog (though make sure it isn't too enthusiastically), and the dog becomes the farmer for the next round.

A-Hunting We Will Go

Number: any number over 8   *Age:* 4–6   *Time:* 2–3 minutes per round   *Adult supervision:* leading singing (if necessary)

Two of the players are chosen as lambs and another is selected to be the fox. The others join hands to form a circle round the fox, and skip round while singing:

> A-Hunting we will go,
> A-Hunting we will go,
> We'll catch a fox
> And put him in a box,
> And never let him go.

During the singing the lambs, who have remained outside the circle, come as close as they dare to tease the fox to chase after them. If the fox breaks out, the lambs dash for safety (and they have one safe place – touching the opposite wall, maybe) where they can't be caught. If the fox *does* catch one of the lambs, that player then becomes the fox and one of the players from the circle becomes a lamb.

Zoo Twins

Number: any even number   *Age:* 3–6   *Time:* 1–2 minutes
Adult supervision: preparing game and helping with pairing if difficulties arise in identification!   (*Equipment:* slips of paper or cards with pictures and names of various animals)

This simple animal game suits both readers and non-readers, but be warned, it can be a noisy experience!
Prepare your set of cards or slips of paper before the game begins. Either draw a picture or stick a photograph or drawing of a zoo animal on each of the cards and write the animal's name underneath. You will need two of each animal. Shuffle the cards and offer them to the players who take one each. Every player has to identify their zoo animal either from the name or the picture, and then start making the animal's noise. You might have monkeys, tigers, parrots, lions, elephants and donkeys prowling round your sitting-room. It doesn't matter what animals are there, because the aim of the game is simply to pair them up. Each of the players listens to the noise made by the other 'animals' and moves over to join his or her partner.

Pat-a-Cake

Number: any number   *Age:* 3–6   *Time:* 1–2 minutes
Adult supervision: leading the singing (if necessary)

Stand the players in front of you, so that they can all see what you are doing. It might be a good idea to run through the words of the song before you start; that will give everyone a chance to find out what is going on. Once the players are ready, start the singing and mime the actions to the words:

Pat-a-cake, pat-a-cake, baker's man
(Clapping hands)
Bake me a cake as fast as you can
(Rolling dough and putting cake in a mould)
Pat it and prick it, and mark it with 'B'
(Patting cake inside mould, pricking cake and
writing 'B' in the air with one finger)
And bake in the oven for baby and me.
(Placing cake in the oven and closing oven door)

Three Blind Mice

Number: any number   *Age:* 3–6   *Time:* 1–2 minutes
Adult supervision: leading singing (if necessary)

You don't have to limit this game to the three mice and the farmer's wife,
any number of players can take part, though for each round you will
need to pick one player to stand in the middle of the circle as the farmer's
wife.

The others join hands to dance round and sing:

Three blind mice,
Three blind mice,
See how they run,
See how they run.
They all ran after the farmer's wife
Who cut off their tails with a carving knife.
Did you ever see such a thing in your life
As three blind mice?

As they sing the last word 'mice', the children let go of each other's
hands and run for their 'hole', a place of safety like a wall or touching a
settee. The farmer's wife has to try and catch one of the players before he
or she reaches the 'hole'. Any mouse caught becomes the farmer's wife in
the next round.

Daylight Robbery *

Number: any number   *Age:* 3–6   *Time:* 3–5 minutes
Adult supervision: preparing loot and judging game
(*Equipment:* an assortment of small objects to act as loot)

Divide the players into two teams and tell them to line up at either end of the playing area. Place the loot in the middle of the room; this should consist of small objects like toys, children's building bricks, fruit and other odds and ends. (There should be ten or twelve times as many objects as there are players on one side – more if you can manage it.)

When the loot is ready, the 'robbery' can begin. On the word 'Go!' all the players rush towards the pile of loot and each takes one object which they carry back to their lair. Then they dash back for another piece of booty and so on until the pile has been cleared. The team with the most loot is the winner.

Busy Bees

Number: any odd number   *Age:* 3–6   *Time:* 1–2 minutes
Adult supervision: seeing that none of the bees crash into anything as they buzz about

A leader is picked and the other children form pairs. The leader calls out different instructions which the pairs obey. 'Stand facing each other' calls the leader; 'Hold left hands'; 'Hold right hands'; 'Kneel back to back' – the leader gives whatever instructions he or she likes. When 'Busy Bees' is called, though, the players suddenly start buzzing round the room looking for a new partner. The leader also tries to grab a partner during the buzzing, and if he or she is successful the odd player out becomes the leader for the next round.

Here We Come Gathering Nuts in May *

Number: any number   *Age:* 3–6   *Time:* 3–5 minutes
Adult supervision: leading the singing and making sure the
tugs-of-war are not too violent   (*Equipment:* cord or old sheet
for tug-of-war)

Two teams are formed, the sheet or cord is laid in the middle of the
playing area and the teams line up facing each other on either side of it.
The game begins with one side joining hands and walking up to the
centre line and back as they sing:

> Here we come gathering nuts in May, nuts in May, nuts in May,
> Here we come gathering nuts in May, on a cold and frosty
>   morning.

Then the other side joins hands and walks up to the centre and back
again also singing:

> Whom will you have for nuts in May, nuts in May, nuts in May,
> Whom will you have for nuts in May, on a cold and frosty
>   morning?

The first side now says who it will have, walking forwards and back
again singing:

> We will have (*name*) for nuts in May, nuts in May, nuts in May,
> We will have (*name*) for nuts in May, on a cold and frosty
>   morning.

The second side replies:

> And whom will you have to fetch her (him) away, fetch her
>   away, fetch her away,
> And whom will you have to fetch her away on a cold and frosty
>   morning?

The first team answers:

> We'll send (*name*) to fetch her away, fetch her away, fetch her
>   away,
> We'll send (*name*) to fetch her away, on a cold and frosty
>   morning.

Now that the two players have been named they have a tug-of-war with
the sheet or cord, with the loser joining the winning side. The game
continues like this until one side loses all its players.

Choo-Choo Tag

Number: any odd number   *Age:* 3–6   *Time:* 3–5 minutes
Adult supervision: preventing game from being too boisterous

One player is picked as the guard, and the rest form pairs. One player in each pair is the engine, the other the coach. Coaches hold engines round the waist and the little trains trundle round the room, trying to keep out of the way of the guard who has missed his own train and is trying to catch another! The guard can only catch a train by catching the coach around the waist. If he (or she) manages to do this, the engine drops out and becomes the guard in the next round.

QUICK AND EASY

Flap Ears

Number: any number   *Age:* 6 upwards   *Length:* 2–3 minutes
Adult supervision: only to see that rules are followed

One player stands in the centre of a circle formed by the others who face inwards. The players in the circle all hold their hands by their ears, palms facing forwards, fingers pointing up. When the player in the middle has his or her back to them, the players flap their fingers like elephants' ears blowing in a strong wind. But as soon as the player in the middle turns towards them, the players must stop flapping and must keep their hands perfectly still.

If the player in the middle catches anyone flapping their fingers, the two players change places. The player in the middle can turn round at any speed and can move in any direction, which keeps the others on their toes.

Fizz-Buzz *

Number: any number   *Age:* 7 upwards   *Time:* 3–5 minutes
Adult supervision: checking on multiples of 3 and 5 in counting

Fizz-Buzz is a daft counting game, ideal for a quiet giggle after everyone has been charging about. The players take it in turns to start counting from 1, replacing every multiple of 3 with 'Fizz', every multiple of 5 with 'Buzz' and every multiple of the two with 'Fizz-Buzz'.

So the first player begins with 'One'. 'Two' says the second player, 'Fizz' says the third, 'Four' says the fourth, 'Buzz' goes the fifth, 'Fizz' shouts the sixth and so on, through 15, which is the first 'Fizz-Buzz', and on up the number ladder. Any player who fails to replace a multiple with 'Fizz', 'Buzz', or 'Fizz-Buzz' drops out, as does anyone who gets their sums wrong and slots in a 'Fizz', 'Buzz' or 'Fizz-Buzz' in the wrong place! The last player left in the game wins.

Who Leads?

Number: any number   *Age:* 7 upwards   *Time:* 2–3 minutes
Adult supervision: only to explain game and call time

The game begins with one player leaving the room. Those remaining sit in a circle and choose a leader who they must all follow. It's the leader's job to start simple movements like patting the head, winking one eye, twiddling thumbs or crossing and uncrossing arms, movements which all other players in the circle have to copy, changing from one to another whenever the leader changes. The aim of the game is for the changes to take place so smoothly that it's very hard to tell who actually gives the lead.

The circle should all be doing one movement when the player outside the room re-enters. He or she has two or three minutes to identify the leader. The leader will obviously try and change the movements when the player from outside is looking away, so it's up to that player to keep darting glances all round the group to spot who makes the changes. If the player from outside spots the leader, they swap places. If he or she hasn't found the leader after the allotted time, tell him or her who it is and send another player outside, picking a new leader for the next round.

Lemon Relay *

Number: any even number   *Age:* 6 upwards   *Time:* 2–3
minutes   *Adult supervision:* umpiring   (*Equipment:* 2 lemons,
2 pencils (plus spares))

Most relay races rely on speed, and speed has a part to play in this one.
What really counts, though, is skill – the skill to roll a lemon from one
side of a room to the other and back again using only a pointed pencil.

Two teams are formed and lined up one player behind the other on
the starting line. The first player in each team is given a lemon and a
pencil. On the word 'Go!' they have to roll their lemons across the room
and back again with the pencil. When they cross the starting line again
they hand the pencil over to the second member who repeats the process.
The relay passes down the team and the first team to have the lemon
rolled home are the winners.

(If you can avoid having to give a demonstration, you'll spare your
blushes!)

Break Out

Number: any number   *Age:* 7 upwards   *Time:* 3–5 minutes
Adult supervision: only to start game and make sure no one
moves feet or legs   (*Equipment:* tennis ball or similar sized
object)

Whoever thought up this game knew the problems of trying to play Tag
in a small space. This tag game is every bit as exciting and challenging as
others but it has the added challenge that players may not move their feet
or legs!

The game begins with players standing in a circle holding hands;
this spaces them correctly. They drop hands and now hold them open
behind their backs. Walk round behind the circle with the tennis ball
and drop it into one player's hands. The player with the ball has to try
and run from the circle before being tagged by the players on either side.
These players can bend and turn as far as they like from the waist up, but
they must not move their feet or legs to catch the player with the ball.

If one is quick enough and tags the quarry, he or she becomes the
player walking round the circle with the ball in the next round.

Rattle Catcher

Number: any number   *Age:* 7 upwards   *Time:* 3–5 minutes
Adult supervision: umpiring and changing players
(*Equipment:* small tin containing a few buttons or similar
objects to make it rattle, blindfold)

One player is blindfolded and stands in the middle of a circle formed by
the other players. The rattle is given to one player in the circle and the
blindfolded player is pointed towards that player. Then the game
begins. The player with the rattle throws it to one of the others in the
circle, who catches it and rattles it, before quickly throwing it to another
player, and so on round the circle. The blindfolded player must try and
keep track of the rattle, with the aim of pointing to the player who is
holding the rattle at any particular time. When he or she does this, the
two players change places and the one caught with the rattle is blindfolded for a turn in the middle.

Card Targets *

Number: any number   *Age:* 6 upwards   *Time:* 2–3 minutes
Adult supervision: only to demonstrate the theory (if not the
practice) and to set throwing distances
(*Equipment:* 10 playing cards per player, washing-up bowl)

Position the players about 3 metres (10 feet) from the washing-up bowl
which is their target. Give each player ten playing cards and tell them
they have to throw and flick the cards into the bowl. Players may develop
whatever method they like to land cards in the target, but the one with
the greatest number of hits is the winner.

King of the Castle

Number: any number   *Age:* 5 upwards   *Time:* 5 minutes
Adult supervision: preventing game from becoming too rough
(*Equipment:* a newspaper)

Although best played outside on grass, this is one of those rough-and-
tumble games that can be played inside without too great a risk to life,
limb and property! Clear a reasonable area and place the newspaper on

the floor as the castle. One player starts by standing on the newspaper and announcing 'I am the King of the Castle'. This is an open challenge to the other players to try and pull him off by overbalancing, rather than excessive violence. Whoever removes the king from his castle takes his place.

Gora *

Number: any number   *Age:* 8 upwards   *Time:* 1–2 minutes per round   *Adult supervision:* only necessary to prevent enthusiasm straying into violence!

This game comes from India where it has been played by children for centuries. The players divide into two teams and toss a coin to see which team will play first. A finishing line is agreed at one end of the playing area. The losing team spread out between the middle of the playing area and the finishing line. The other team line up side by side in the middle of the playing area and link arms, with the leader in the middle. While the leader stands still the other players revolve in a circle, like a spoke in a wheel. As they rotate, the players chant 'Go-ra', 'Go-ra' until the leader suddenly shouts 'Off!' The players break away and run as fast as they can to the finishing line without being touched by any of the other team. When all the players have either reached safety or have been caught, it's the turn of the other team to form a 'wheel' and chant 'Go-ra'.

Giant's Steps *

Number: any even number   *Age:* 7 upwards   *Time:* 2–3 minutes   *Adult supervision:* judging progress of both teams

The players form two teams which line up, with the leader at the head and the rest of the team one behind the other, at the starting line.

When the game begins the leaders step out as far as they can reach. The second player in each team then starts from the point reached by the first and again steps out as far as he or she can reach. The third player does the same and so do all the others until everyone in the team has tried stepping a 'giant's step'. The team which has reached the point furthest from the starting line wins the game, so it's obviously a game in which tall players come into their own!

Up and Over Down and Under *

Number: any even number   *Age:* 7 upwards   *Time:* 2–3
minutes   *Adult supervision:* judging racing

Two teams are formed and they line up side by side with one player
standing 2 metres (6 feet) in front of the one behind. On the word 'Go!'
the rear man in each team leapfrogs the player in front, crawls under the
legs of the one in front of him, leapfrogs the next and so on up the line.
When he reaches the front he runs to the back and touches the next
player on the shoulder who alternately leapfrogs and crawls his way up
the line before returning to his original place and sending the next
player on his way. The first team to complete the relay wins the race.

Jousting *

Number: any even number   *Age:* 9 upwards   *Time:* 5–10
minutes   *Adult supervision:* making sure there is more tumble
than rough

This is a boys' game to be played on grass where the 'riders' and their
'mounts' can fall without hurting themselves. The boys divide into pairs
and one carries the other piggyback, forming a jousting combination of
rider and horse. Two pairs 'clash' in the first round with the aim being to
force the opposing pair to fall or lose the rider. The winning pair takes on
the next challenger and the game continues like this until everyone has
competed. The jousting pair with the highest number of victories is the
winner.

Stretch and Bend

Number: any number   *Age:* 6 upwards   *Time:* 2–3 minutes
Adult supervision: either leading the game (if it isn't too
energetic) or catching out players

A leader (if it isn't you) is picked and stands in the middle of a circle formed
by the others. The leader tells the others either to 'Stretch' or 'Bend'.
However, they have to follow what the leader *does*, not what is said!
   'Stretch', says the leader standing upright as tall as possible. 'Bend',
he says, bending down. 'Stretch', standing up again. 'Bend', he says, but
remains standing up. Any player who does bend drops out.

The game is the greatest fun when played at a furious pace, so it's up to the leader to get the game moving as fast as possible, particularly with the die-hard players who last out to the end!

Fire! Fire! *

Number: any even number   *Age:* 5–9   *Time:* 3–5 minutes
Adult supervision: explaining rules and judging contents
of saucepan   (*Equipment:* 2 buckets filled with water, 2 equal-sized saucepans and 2 equal-sized cups)

Two teams are formed and line up, one player behind the other. The buckets of water are placed in front of the first player in each team and the saucepans are put behind the last. The first player in each team is given a cup, and on the word 'Fire!' scoops a cupful of water from the bucket and passes the cup down the line, from player to player, until it reaches the last one who pours the water (or what is left of it) into the saucepan. The cup is passed back up the line to the first player who refills it and sends it back to the saucepan as before. This carries on until the saucepan is filled, with the winning team being the one to fill its saucepan first, and put out the fire.

Dragon Heads and Tails

Number: any number   *Age:* 5 upwards   *Time:* 2–3 minutes
Adult supervision: only to explain rules and judge the play
(if necessary)

In China, where this game originates, dragons have great spiritual significance and feature in many Chinese festivals and celebrations. In this game the children line up, each holding the shoulders of the one in front, to form a dragon. The child at the front of the line is the dragon's head; the one at the end, its tail.

The game begins with the dragon in a straight line, standing quite still; it's asleep. It wakes up when one of the players in the middle of the body shouts 'Chase'. At this the head whips round and starts chasing the tail, which in turn tries to keep out of its way. The fun of the game is that *the body must stay together* while this chasing takes place; none of the players may let go of the shoulders of the one in front.

If the head manages to touch the tail, he or she stays as the head for the next round. If the dragon line breaks during the chase, then the head goes down to the tail and the second player in the line becomes the head. This process carries on through the game until every child in the dragon's body has had a go at being the head.

Roundabout Escape

Number: any number   *Age:* 5 upwards   *Time:* 5 minutes
Adult supervision: watching for false touches

One player is chosen as 'It' and stands outside a circle formed by the other players joining hands. When the game begins, It names one of the players in the circle and then tries to catch him or her. The named player tries to keep out of It's reach, helped by the rest of the circle. The circle must stay joined the whole time, but the named player may pull the others first one way and then the other to keep out of It's way. If It touches the wrong player twice, he or she is replaced by a player from the circle. If It is successful, he or she remains It for the next round.

Balloon Buffeting *

Number: any even number   *Age:* 8 upwards   *Time:* 5–10 minutes   *Adult supervision:* tossing balloon to players and keeping score   *(Equipment:* an inflated balloon, (spares))

This game comes from the USA where it is known by a variety of names. The players divide into two teams and sit down facing one another. Everyone stretches out their legs so that the soles of their shoes are pressed against those of the player opposite. Everyone then puts their left hands behind their backs and must keep them there for the rest of the game!

The game is like volley ball, but is played with one hand and seated. The balloon is thrown between the two lines and players try to hit it with their right hands as soon as it comes within range; the aim of the game is to score a point by knocking the balloon over the heads of the other team. When this happens the balloon is thrown between the rows to start play once more.

The winning team is the one with the highest score at the end of time.

WORD GAMES

Coffee Pot

Number: any number   *Age:* 8 upwards   *Time:* 2–3 minutes
Adult supervision: only to make sure that 'coffee pot' is used
in the right context

One player leaves the room while all the others think of a secret word.
When this has been chosen the player outside is called in again. He or
she has to discover the secret word by asking questions to which the
others reply. Every reply must contain the secret word but in a disguised
form – the words *coffee pot* are used in its place. This can lead to some
extraordinary conversations as this possibility shows (the secret word is
boat):

> Question: 'Did you watch television last night?'
> Answer: 'No, I was busy in my room building a model *coffee
>   pot.*'
> Question: 'What's your favourite colour?'
> Answer: 'I like the blue which they use to paint the *coffee pots*
>   you can hire in the park.'
> Question: 'Where do you live?'
> Answer: 'In the road that was flooded so badly two winters ago
>   that we had to be rescued by soldiers who arrived at the door
>   in a *coffee pot.*'

Word Chains *

Number: any number   *Age:* 8 upwards   *Time:* 5–10 minutes
Adult supervision: only to check that one word follows the
other according to the rules

The players sit down in a circle and one player chooses a word which he
or she says aloud. The player sitting on the first player's left must now
think of a word that begins with the last syllable of the previous word.
Supposing the first word was 'Unite', the second word might be 'Item'.
The next player on the left now has to think of a word beginning with
'em', and he or she may say 'Empty'. The fourth player suggests 'Type'.

But the fifth player can't think of a word within the thirty second limit, and drops out of the game. The next player to the left starts the game again with another word. No words that have been used already in a round may be used again. The last player left in the game is the winner.

Minute Words

Number: any number   *Age:* 7 upwards   *Time:* 1 minute per player per turn   *Adult supervision:* only to explain rules and keep count of words (if necessary)   (*Equipment:* means of keeping time)

The players sit in a circle, and the group leader points to one of them and names a letter of the alphabet. That player then has one minute to rattle off as many words beginning with that letter as he or she can think of. When the minute is up, that player points to someone else and calls another letter.

Although this sounds too simple, it's surprising how difficult calling the words can be, even with letters for which you would expect there to be dozens of possibilities. The game ends when everyone has had a go.

A Was an Apple Pie

Number: any number   *Age:* 8 upwards   *Time:* 2–3 minutes
Adult supervision: only to explain rules

The players sit in a circle, and one after the other name verbs in alphabetical order (leaving out difficult letters like Z, X, Q and possibly K). The first player starts the game with the phrase 'A was an apple pie. A *ate* it.' The second player continues 'B *bought* it'. 'C *collected* it,' says the third. The fourth adds 'D *delivered* it' – and so on through the alphabet. There is no need to repeat the first phrase ('A was an apple pie'), but if the game starts another full circle with A again, players must not repeat verbs already used.

Famous Fives *

Number: any number   *Age:* 8 upwards   *Time:* 5–10 minutes
Adult supervision: explaining game and possibly acting as
questioner

The players sit in a line and the questioner walks along asking them in
turn to name a group of five objects. 'Name five football teams', 'Name
five famous singers', 'Name five towns by the sea', 'Name five breeds of
dog' – these are the sort of questions that might be asked. Players score
one point for each correct object they name. If they name all five, they
score a bonus of ten points. But they lose two points for every incorrect
answer. Play the game for five rounds. The player with the highest score
at the end wins the game.

I Love My Love *

Number: any number   *Age:* 7 upwards   *Time:* 2–3 minutes
Adult supervision: only to explain rules and help where needed

This well-tried old favourite is a game which children adore playing.
Like many alphabet games the players have to work their way through
from A to Z (though Z and X are often left out) finding adjectives to
describe 'My Love'.

The first player might begin, 'I love my love because he/she is
artistic.' Then comes the second player who says, 'I love my love because
he/she is brave.' The others follow on with the game, going round the
group until one player gets stuck and can't think of a word that will fit.
When this happens the player drops out and the next one starts again
with A, though all the players must think of *new words*. A player who
repeats an adjective that has been used already leaves the game.

The last player left in the group is the winner.

Tourist Trail

Number: any number   *Age:* 8 upwards   *Time:* 3–5 minutes
Adult supervision: only to explain rules and keep time
(*Equipment:* means of keeping time)

All the players but one sit in a circle, and the odd one out starts the game as the man-in-the-middle. He or she points to one of the circle of players and says, for example, 'I am going to London.' The player pointed at now has ten seconds to say three nouns that begin with the same initial as the destination mentioned; so in this case he or she might answer, 'Lunch, licence, lamb'. Then it's that player's turn to point to someone else and call a destination. If anyone can't manage to think of three nouns in the time, he or she changes places with the man-in-the-middle. Anyone who suggests going to Zomba or Zaire, or anywhere else beginning with an impossibly difficult letter should be made to stay in the middle for an extra round, even if the player pointed at does manage to answer 'Zoo, zero and zinc' in time!

Consonant Catalogue *

Number: any number   *Age:* 5 upwards   *Time:* 3–5 minutes
Adult supervision: only to explain rules and check that the vowels are omitted   (*Equipment:* means of keeping time accurately (ideally a stopwatch))

The players sit in a circle and take it in turns to recite the alphabet from B to Z, leaving out all the vowels. The player who does this in the fastest time wins the game. Any vowels included by mistake carry a penalty of five seconds each.

Try repeating the alphabet like this yourself and you'll find it's not as easy as it may sound: BCDFGHJKLMNPQRSTVWXYZ!

Animal, Vegetable, or Mineral

Number: any number   *Age:* 8 upwards   *Time:* 2–3 minutes
Adult supervision: explaining rules and keeping time

This is one of the most popular traditional word games around. It involves everyone all the time, and appeals to the players' imagination as well as their powers of questioning and deduction.

One player thinks of a subject which the others have to guess. They may ask any questions that call for simple 'Yes' or 'No' answers. On the basis of the answers they get, they narrow down the field until one of them discovers the subject the player has thought of.

The game gets its name from the first question which is always 'Animal, vegetable, or mineral'. If the subject is 'Gold', the player answers 'Mineral', which immediately rules out every animal from Apes to Zebras, via Man and Marsupials, as well as excluding any ideas about plants ranging from Artichokes to Zebrinas. From then on the players fire questions, trying to prise information from the player who guards the secret to the subject. He or she must reply truthfully to the questions but need only answer 'Yes' or 'No'. There need not be any time limit on the game, provided that the questions are fired thick and fast, but if it looks as if the players are totally at sea, ask what the subject is and then give another player a chance to think of one.

Who Am I?

Number: any number   *Age:* 8 upwards   *Time:* 5 minutes or
longer   *Adult supervision:* preparing name sheets
(*Equipment:* one slip of paper and a safety-pin per player)

Write the names of famous people of fact and fiction, both funny and serious, on the slips of paper and pin one name to the back of every player, without any of the players seeing who he or she is! (Hide all the mirrors just in case.) The game is spent with the players trying to find out who they are by asking each other questions. The only questions allowed are those that require simple 'Yes' or 'No' answers. The more entertaining you can make your range of names, the more fun the players will have discovering their own identities.

Spelling Bee *

Number: any number   *Age:* 7 upwards   *Time:* 5 minutes
Adult supervision: explaining game and possibly acting as
question master   (*Equipment:* children's dictionary)

The players sit in a circle round the questioner who asks each in turn to
spell a word. The questioner must pitch words at the level of the players,
which requires some skill. The children's dictionary will be helpful in
the first selection of words, but the questioner will have to decide how
difficult to make the words to suit individual children.

A child who spells a word correctly scores one point. A child who
spells one incorrectly loses a point. Play the game for a set number of
rounds (lasting about five minutes altogether), and the player who has
the highest score at the end is the winner.

Capital Catching *

Number: any number   *Age:* 8 upwards   *Time:* 2–3 minutes
Adult supervision: only to make sure that the cities called are
in fact capitals   (*Equipment:* 1 ball)

The players sit in a circle and one is given the ball. The game begins with
the ball being thrown to another player who catches it and has to name a
capital city at the same time. He or she then throws the ball to another
player, who catches it and names another capital, and so on. Players who
either drop the ball, name a capital that has already been named, or fail to
name one at all, leave the circle. The last one left catching the ball and
naming a new capital is the winner.

Sentences

Number: any number   *Age:* 7 upwards   *Time:* 2–3 minutes per
round   *Adult supervision:* only to see that each sentence has
words beginning with the right letters

The game begins with one player choosing a word. It can be any word he
or she likes, but one with five or more letters makes the game more fun.
The word is announced to all the other players who then make sentences. Each word of the sentence must begin with, and be in the same

order as, each letter of the chosen word, so that there are the same number of words in the sentence as there are letters in the chosen word. So if the chosen word was 'Summer', one player might produce the sentence: 'School uniform makes me extremely red!' which may not make much sense, but does follow the rules of the game.

Traveller's Tales *

Number: any number   *Age:* 8 upwards   *Time:* 3–5 minutes per round   *Adult supervision:* only to explain the game

Every player is a traveller with the world at his feet. They sit in a circle and each in turn asks two questions of the player to the right. In reply, the first player names a destination that begins with the first letter of the alphabet (the second player names one beginning with B and so on). The second question is trickier. Here the player answering must produce a three-letter sentence with words that each begin with the same letter as the destination. In each case the questions asked follow the same pattern, and a typical exchange might go like this:

> Susan: 'Where are you going?'
> Peter: 'Africa'
> Susan: 'What will you do there?'
> Peter: 'Assist aged apes.'
> Peter: 'Where are you going?'
> George: 'Bolivia.'
> Peter: 'What will you do there?'
> George: 'Bury beer bottles!'

Any player who can't think of a suitable reply after twenty seconds must leave the circle. The last one left in is the winner.

Rhyme Counting *

Number: any number   *Age:* 8 upwards   *Time:* 2–3 minutes per round   *Adult supervision:* only to explain game and give a helpful hint to any players having real problems!

This is a counting game with a difference. The players start counting at 'One' and move up from there, but with every number they count, they must add a word or words that begin with the same initial as the number. So the first player might say 'One ostrich', the second player repeats this and adds a word of his own, saying 'One ostrich, Two twins'. The third player follows, repeating what has gone before and adding his own number and words.

The game progresses like this, with players who make mistakes in the list, or who use words that have already been used, dropping out. The one who is last in adding a number and repeating the list without any mistakes wins the game.

These are some of the rhyme counts you might use:

> One Oar
> Two Tubs
> Three Thrushes
> Four Fine Freckles
> Five Fat Fellows
> Six Sooty Sweeps
> Seven Salt Seas

Tennis, Elbow, Foot *

Number: any number   *Age:* 8 upwards   *Time:* 3–5 minutes per round   *Adult supervision:* only to start game and explain rules

The players sit in a circle and the one who starts the game says a word out loud; in the case of the game's name, he or she says 'Tennis'. The next player to the right must reply immediately with a word that has some connection with this. 'Elbow' is the answer. The next player to the right racks his mind for a word connected with 'elbow', and comes up with an easy one: 'Foot'. And so the game progresses round the circle, with every player to the right thinking up a word connected with the previous one. Anyone who pauses, or who calls a word that has no connection with the previous word leaves the game. The last one left in is the winner.

Word Wise *

Number: any number   *Age:* 8 upwards   *Time:* 1–2 minutes per round   *Adult supervision:* demonstrating game and possibly writing words on board or paper   (*Equipment:* blackboard and chalk or large sheet of paper and pencil)

The game begins with the players sitting on the floor in front of a blackboard or sitting round a large sheet of paper on a table. The leader thinks of a well-known phrase and marks dashes on the board or paper for every letter in the word. The other players must then guess letters that might fit in the phrase. If they are successful, the leader writes the letters in their right place in the phrase, and gives the successful player one point. If a letter does not appear in the phrase, the player who guessed it loses a point. The player who guesses the correct phrase wins five extra points. The player with the most points at the end of each round wins it. Play the game for ten rounds, and if younger children want to play include a clue before the guessing begins. If the phrase was 'Raining cats and dogs', for example, a suitable clue would be 'Bad weather'.

Snip

Number: any number   *Age:* 7 upwards   *Time:* 5–10 minutes
Adult supervision: only to explain rules

Get all the players to sit in a circle except for one who starts in the middle. The game begins with the middleman pointing to one of the players in the circle while pronouncing and spelling a three-letter word. He or she then starts a steady count to 12 before calling 'Snip'. So the player might point to one of the others and say: 'Pit, P-I-T, 1-2-3-4-5-6-7-8-9-10-11-12, Snip!'

During the counting the player pointed at has to think of three words that begin with the three letters in the word spelt out. These can be any words (names are allowed, too), but they must be said before the word 'Snip' cuts off the flow. In the case of 'Pit', then, the player might answer 'Pig', 'Ink' and 'Tractor'. There is no limitation on the words used, provided they begin with the right letters and are in the right order. Any player who fails to come up with three words in the time limit swaps places with the middleman.

ZYX *

Number: any number   *Age:* 5 upwards   *Time:* 3–5 minutes
Adult supervision: timing game and keeping check on alphabet
(*Equipment:* means of keeping time accurately (ideally
a stopwatch))

The players sit in a circle and take it in turns to repeat the alphabet
backwards from Z to A. The one who repeats it fastest is the winner.
However, repeating the alphabet backwards is easy enough in theory,
but in practice it is pretty difficult. Any mistakes carry a penalty of five
seconds, so players who think before they speak stand a better chance of
getting the letters in the right order than those who race through too fast
and get several letters in the wrong place. The stopwatch or other clock
records the times to the nearest second.

PAPER AND PENCIL GAMES

*Equipment: Pencils and paper are needed for all games in this
section.*

Hangman

Number: any number   *Age:* 7 upwards   *Time:* 5 minutes
Adult supervision: only to explain rules and possibly set words

This popular spelling game has been around for years and is ideal for
children of any age because the difficulty of the words can be matched to
the children's spelling ability.

One player thinks of a word (usually with about five or six letters).
He or she marks one dash for every letter in the word. The other players
take it in turns to guess letters which might be in the secret word. If a
guess is successful, the letter is marked over the dash that represents it,
though if the same letter appears again in the word it is still written in
only once and has to be guessed again to appear elsewhere. If a player
makes a wrong guess, that letter is written under the line of dashes and
the first part of the *Hangman* picture is drawn, the line representing the
ground in which the gibbet stands. The game continues round the group
with each player taking it in turns to guess a letter. If the secret word is

discovered before the 'hanging' is completed, another player chooses a secret word for the next round. If the 'hanging' takes place before the word is discovered, then the same player chooses another word.

Battleships *

Number: 2   *Age:* 7 upwards   *Time:* 5 minutes   *Adult supervision:* only necessary to explain rules

It is said that this game was developed by British prisoners-of-war during the First World War. Since then it has become one of the most popular pencil and paper games for two players.

Each player requires ten-by-ten grids. These are most easily drawn on graph paper, but if this is not available the players will need to draw the grids themselves. One grid is marked Home Fleet, the other Enemy Fleet. The squares along the top of the grids run from left to right and are lettered A to J, the squares down the lefthand side are numbered 1 to 10.

Both players keep their papers hidden because each will position his own ships in the grid marked Home Fleet. He may position his fleet wherever he likes in the grid. A fleet consists of:

> one battleship (4 squares long)
> two cruisers (3 squares long each)
> three destroyers (2 squares long each)
> four submarines (one square long each)

A player positions his fleet by outlining the appropriate number of squares in vertical or horizontal rows, with at least one vacant square between ships.

The players toss a coin to decide who will open the battle, and the winner fires the opening shots by calling three squares. He calls the letters and numbers one at a time, pinpointing the squares he is attacking. As he does this he marks his grid named Enemy Fleet, to keep a record of his shots. His opponent must tell him whether or not these shots scored hits, and if they did he must state what type of ship was hit. A ship can only be sunk when all of its squares have been hit.

The game continues with the players taking it in turns to fire three shots at their opponent's fleet and then marking the results on their respective grids, with the aim always being to sink an enemy fleet before it sinks your own!

The winner destroys the enemy fleet first, as might be expected.

A possible sheet for Battleships might look like this:

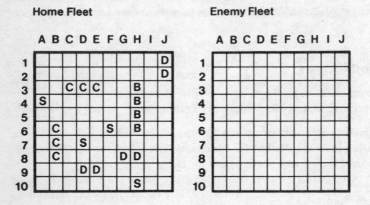

Home Fleet   **Enemy Fleet**

Boxes *

Number: 2   *Age:* 6 upwards   *Time:* 2–3 minutes
Adult supervision: only to explain rules

One of the players marks any number of dots on a sheet of paper. These are marked in rows, and a normal arrangement is ten rows of ten dots. Then, taking it in turns, the players draw horizontal or vertical lines to join any two dots that are next to each other (diagonal lines are not allowed).

The aim of the game is to complete as many boxes (squares) as possible, by drawing the last line to each one. When a player manages to do this, ho initials the box and then draws another line. His turn continues until he draws a line which does not complete a box. When all the boxes have been filled, the player with the highest number wins.

The skill in the game lies in drawing lines that prevent your opponent from completing too many boxes, but which will help you complete masses when your own chance comes!

News Line *

Number: any number   *Age:* 4 upwards   *Time:* 1–2 minutes
Adult supervision: judging results   (*Equipment:* equal columns of newsprint)

Get all the players to sit somewhere where they can press on a surface. Give each one a pencil and a column of newsprint (all columns of the same length). On the word 'Go!' every player must draw a line under the top line of print and then work down the column from right to left and left to right alternately drawing a zigzag line without a break under each of the lines. The first player to complete this accurately without leaving out any lines of print is the winner.

Mirror Images

Number: any number   *Age:* 6 upwards   *Time:* 5–10 minutes
Adult supervision: checking that no one cheats and looks at the paper   (*Equipment:* a mirror)

Unless you have several mirrors available, this is a game which players will tackle one at a time, but that doesn't prevent everyone else from watching and making sure there is no cheating, because in this game the temptation to cheat is very strong!

Sit the player who is going to draw at a table in front of a mirror, so that he or she can see clearly the reflection of the sheet of paper on which the drawing will be made. Now without looking down at the paper, but concentrating solely on the reflection in the mirror, the player has to draw a simple object; you might suggest a sailing boat, a house or a car. Even with objects like these it is very difficult to draw accurately using only a reflection. Try it yourself and see!

Join the Numbers *

Number: 2   *Age:* 5 upwards   *Time:* 2–3 minutes
Adult supervision: only to explain rules

The first player picks up a pencil and writes the numbers 1 to 21 higgledy-piggledy all over the paper. Then the second player repeats each of the numbers in the same way, making sure that one number does not come too close to its twin, so that the paper is filled with a random arrangement of 42 numbers in all.

The players then toss a coin to see who will start the game, the aim being to join two of the same numbers. So one player may join the two 2s, the other may join the two 17s and so on. The one snag is that in joining a pair of numbers, no player may cross a line already drawn between two other numbers. They take it in turns to link the numbers until one of them is stuck and cannot draw a line in any direction to link any pairs. When this happens the other player is the winner.

Guess in the Dark *

Number: any number   *Age:* 7 upwards   *Time:* 3–5 minutes
Adult supervision: preparing objects for passing round
(*Equipment:* ten objects)

All the players sit round a table, each with a paper and pencil. The light is turned out, the curtains drawn, so that the room is pitch black. The first mystery object is passed round the group and the players have to identify this by touch only. When everyone has handled the object and it has been returned, and hidden from sight, the light is turned on and each player writes down what he or she thinks the object is. Then the lights are turned out and the next object is passed round as before. Ten objects are passed round altogether, objects like: a potato; a yoyo; a kitchen scourer; an eraser; an orange; a hair-clip.

The player who has named the greatest number of mystery objects is the winner.

First Names First *

Number: any number   *Age:* 7 upwards   *Time:* 5–10 minutes
Adult supervision: choosing name and judging answers

Seat all the players where they can write and give each one a sheet of paper and a pencil. Then tell them the name you have chosen. This should be a fairly long name, like Nichola, for example. Ask them to write this across the top of their paper, and then tell them to list as many names as they can beneath each of the letters (all of the names beginning with that letter). So all the names beginning with N go under N, all those beginning with L go under L, and so on. Tell them how many minutes they have to compile the list, and when the time is up, whosever list is the longest (and the most accurate) is the winner.

In the case of Nichola a typical list might start like this:

N	I	C	H	O	L	A
Nina	Ian	Colin	Henry	Oliver	Leonard	Alan
Nancy		Charles	Hugh	Olivia	Lawrence	Anne
Nigel		Christopher	Herbert	Octavia	Leo	Anita
Nevil		Carol	Harold		Lindsay	Andrew
Noel		Christina	Hannah		Lucy	Arthur
Nicholas		Claire			Linda	

Squaring Up *

Number: 2   *Age:* 7 upwards   *Time:* 3–5 minutes
Adult supervision: only to explain rules

The game begins with one of the players drawing a grid of squares, the same number on each side. At first it is a good idea to limit the game to no more than 7 squares to a side, but when the players have more experience, more squares can be added to make the game more challenging.

When the grid is ready, the players toss a coin to see who will start and the first one marks one of the squares with his or her initial. The other player does the same and they take it in turns marking the squares with the idea of completing a line of squares from one side of the grid to the other. These must be straight lines, running vertically, horizontally, or diagonally. A player who completes a line scores as many points as there are squares in the line. If he or she actually completes more than one line – perhaps a diagonal line and a vertical one meet at the same square – the total number of squares in both lines is added to the player's score. The player who finishes a line gets an extra turn, and can carry on playing until there are no more convenient lines to complete. The player with the highest number of points when all the squares have been filled is the winner.

The Worm *

Number: 2   *Age:* 6 upwards   *Time:* 2–3 minutes
Adult supervision: only to explain rules

The game begins with ten rows of ten dots being marked on a sheet of paper. The players toss a coin to see who will start, and the winner draws a line vertically or horizontally to join two dots next to each other (diagonal lines are not allowed). The second player takes the pencil and draws another vertical or horizontal line joining one end of the first line. The game continues with the players taking it in turns to draw lines like this, adding to either end of the existing line or 'worm'. The aim of each player is to force the other into such a position that he or she can only draw a line which will join up with the main body of the worm, so losing the game.

In the game below the next player to play must lose because he can only draw lines that will connect one end or the other to the rest of the 'worm'.

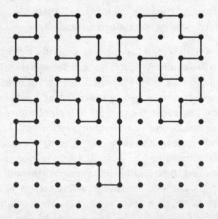

Picture Consequences

Number: any number over 4 *Age:* 5 upwards *Time:* 2–3 minutes *Adult supervision:* only to explain rules and judge results

The players sit in a circle round a table, and each draws a face at the top of his or her strip of paper. The players can draw any sort of face they like, just as long as the others don't catch sight of it. When everyone has completed a face, they fold over the top of their piece of paper, hiding the faces, and the strips are passed to the players sitting on the right. Now everyone draws a body on the strip of paper they have received (still without looking at the face above), and a pair of arms as well. Again the paper is folded to hide these and it is passed once more to the right. The next parts to be added are the legs. When these have been drawn, the strips are passed to the right once more for the final addition – the picture's feet.

When all the drawings have been completed, all the strips are gathered in and are unfolded one by one, so that everyone can admire these joint masterpieces and laugh out loud at most of them.

Smell It Out

Number: any number *Age:* 7 upwards *Time:* 5 minutes *Adult supervision:* only to explain rules and prepare samples (*Equipment:* empty jars containing objects to be smelled, blindfolds)

Each of the players is blindfolded, and led over to a row of jars containing a variety of smelly objects. There might be some 'ripe' cheese in one, an onion in another, soap, orange, coffee, tea, shoe polish, or mint in the others (one in each). For fun you might include a non-smelling substance like water in one. Allow each player half a minute to smell each jar, and when everyone has had a smell, cover over the jars, tell the players to remove their blindfolds, and ask them to list the things they have smelled. You may be surprised by some of the things they put down!

Pairing up *

Number: any number   *Age:* 8 upwards   *Time:* 5 minutes
Adult supervision: calling one half of each pair
(Equipment: list of pairs)

Each player is given a pencil and a piece of paper. The leader reads one half of a well-known pair from a prepared list, allowing only a second or two before moving on to the next one. The players have to try and write down as many of the missing words as they can to complete the pairs. The player who writes down the most matching pairs wins.

Suitable pairs might be: Jack . . . and Jill; cats . . . and dogs; David . . . and Goliath; Adam . . . and Eve; bat . . . and ball; sugar . . . and spice, etc.

CARD GAMES

Equipment: A pack of playing cards is needed for all games in this section.

Pelmanism *

Number: 2 or more   *Age:* 7 upwards   *Time:* 5–10 minutes
Adult supervision: explaining rules

This game's other name, *Concentration*, indicates that it is one in which a good memory and close attention to the play pays off. It's an easy game to play, and one which attentive players enjoy greatly. It's also one in which adults and children can compete on almost equal terms.

Take an ordinary pack of 52 cards and lay them out face down on a large table or on the floor. They may be laid in even rows or scattered higgledy-piggledy, the only guideline is that no two cards may touch each other.

Play starts when the first player turns over any two cards, allowing all the players to see them. If the cards have the same value (e.g. two aces) the player keeps them and has another go, turning over two more cards. If the cards have different values the player must replace them face down in the same place that they were picked up. The next player then has a chance to pick any two cards. A player may continue to collect pairs for as long as he or she can. A 'go' only stops when cards that do not have the same value are turned over.

The secret of success in this game is to pay very close attention to the cards turned up by the other players. A player who turns up a 'two' in his own go and can remember where another player turned up a 'two' previously, will be able to make a pair. If he then turns up an 'eight' and recalls that there's another 'eight' across the floor, he's got another pair.

As the game develops and more cards are turned up, the players with the best memories will acquire pairs, sometimes through quite long turns. The game continues until all the cards have been removed from the floor or table, and the player with the greatest number of pairs wins.

Snap *

Number. 2 or more   Age: 4 upwards   Time: 5–10 minutes
Adult supervision: only to explain rules

You can buy special packs of cards for Snap, which appeal to younger players because of their bright designs or pictures, but the game can be played equally well with ordinary playing cards. Use two packs shuffled together if there are more than four players.

The cards are well shuffled and are dealt to the players one at a time face down. If some players get an odd card more than the others, this doesn't matter. Each player then stacks his or her cards into a neat pile face down, without looking at them.

Play begins with the player to the dealer's left turning over his or her top card and placing it face up beside the pile of face-down cards. The next player to the left does likewise. Play carries on in this way with each player turning over the top card and starting a face-up pile. As each player turns the card, all eyes should be glued on it because whenever a player spots that two cards on any of the face-up piles have the same value, he or she can call 'Snap!' and claim both piles, and it's the first player to call 'Snap!' who wins the cards. Concentration counts.

Cards won by calling 'Snap!' are added to the bottom of the face-down piles, and play resumes with the player to the left of the one who called 'Snap!' turning over his next card. A player who has used up his face-down pile can still stay in the game providing he still has a face-up pile. Players in this position pass when their turns come to play cards, but they can still call 'Snap!' when they see pairs on face-up piles. Players who lose both piles must leave the game.

Over-eager players who call 'Snap' by mistake, when there are not two of the same cards showing, must pay a forfeit and hand one card from their face-down pile to each of the other players, who add them to the bottom of their face-down piles. The player who ends up with all the cards is the winner.

Simple variation
Younger players may prefer to play 'Snap' with one central face-up pile instead of individual ones. This makes the game easier and the rules are the same except that the top two cards on the pile must match instead of two on any separate piles. A player who correctly calls 'Snap!' in this game wins all the cards in the central pile.

Old Maid *

Number: 3 or more   *Age:* 5 upwards   *Time:* 3–5 minutes
Adult supervision: only to explain rules

As with many children's card games, you can buy special sets of Old Maid cards, but the game can be played perfectly well with ordinary playing cards, from which one queen has been removed. The object is to get rid of all one's cards and only one player is prevented from doing this – the one with the odd queen, or old maid!

The pack is well shuffled and dealt one card at a time to all the players. Everyone looks at their cards and keeps them well hidden from prying eyes. Play starts with all the players discarding any pairs of cards by placing them face down on the table. Two cards of the same value form a pair, four cards of the same value form two pairs, but three cards of the same value form only one pair, and the odd card must be retained in the hand.

When everyone has discarded pairs, the player to the dealer's left fans out his or her remaining cards and offers them face downwards to the player on the left, who can pick any one he or she likes. If this card forms a pair with one in the player's own hand, that pair joins the others on the table. If it doesn't, it must stay in the hand until the next round. This player then fans out his or her cards and offers them face downwards to the next player on the left, who repeats the procedure. Play continues like this, round and round the group, until every player but one has managed to pair and discard their cards. The one player left holding a card is the one with the old maid (the odd queen).

Snip-Snap-Snorem *

Number: 3 or more   *Age:* 5 upwards   *Time:* 5 minutes
Adult supervision: only to explain rules

One of the players deals the whole pack face down to the others, one card at a time, at the start of this simple but enjoyable family game. The players pick up their cards and look at them, without letting the other players see what they are.

The player on the left of the dealer starts play by placing any one of his or her cards upwards in the centre of the table. If the next player has another card of the same value it should be placed on top with the accompanying announcement 'Snip!'. But if the player's hand doesn't contain a card of the same value, he or she says 'Pass', and the next player has a turn. The next player to play a card of the value of the 'Snip!' card calls 'Snap!', and the one to play the fourth and last card with that value calls 'Snorem!', and starts the next round by playing one of his or her remaining cards. Players who have two cards of the same value in their hand can still play only one at a time, whenever their turn comes round.

All the rounds are played in the same way, with each player trying to be the first to get rid of all of his or her cards. The first player to do this wins the game.

Happy Families *

Number: 3 or more   *Age:* 4 upwards   *Time:* 5–10 minutes
Adult supervision: only to explain rules

Children of all ages enjoy this quiet, simple game, especially if it is played with a special pack of *Happy Families* cards featuring animals or other colourful family groups, but an ordinary pack of cards will do just as well.

Play begins with one player dealing the pack face down to the others one card at a time. The players pick up their cards and, keeping them well hidden, group them into families. There are four cards to each family, usually a mother, father, daughter and son, or, if using ordinary cards, four of the same value. The aim of the game is to complete as many families as possible.

After everyone has arranged their cards, the player on the dealer's left starts the game by asking one of the other players if he or she has a particular card which is needed to help complete a family. Any card may be asked for, as long as the player has at least one card belonging to that family. If the player has the card which is asked for it must be given over, and the asking player may then ask a player for another card. His or her turn continues until a player who is asked for a card does not have that card. When this happens the player who is asked becomes the asker, and can start trying to complete families of his or her own.

A player who completes a family places all four cards face down on the table. At the end of the game, when all the families have been grouped together, the player with the greatest number wins.

Donkey *

Number: 3 or more   *Age:* 6 upwards   *Time:* 3–5 minutes
Adult supervision: only to explain rules

No one wins a game of Donkey, there is only a loser; that is the first player who collects all the letters in DONKEY.

The game can be played easily after only a few trial runs, and is great fun when played as fast as possible. The game is played with one set of cards for each player, a set being four cards of the same value. So six players might use: aces, twos, threes, fours, fives and sixes. These sets are taken from the pack and the rest are put aside. The chosen cards are well shuffled and are dealt to the players face down. The object of the game is either to be the first player to get four cards of the same value, or to avoid being the last one to react when one of the others goes 'out'.

The players pick up their cards and look at them, keeping them hidden from the others. Each player then decides which card he or she does not want, and puts it face down on the table. Then all the players pass their face-down cards to the left at the same time and pick up the cards they have been given, before discarding another card and passing this to the left as before.

The passing continues like this, as fast as possible, until one player manages to get four cards of the same value. He or she quietly puts the cards down on the table and lifts a finger alongside his or her nose. As soon as the other players see this happening, they must put down their own cards and lift a finger to the nose as well. The last player to realize what is going on loses the round, and is penalized with the first letter of Donkey, the D.

The next round is played as before, even faster if possible, and gradually the players build up their Donkeys until one of them is unlucky enough to be penalized with the Y. He or she loses the game and has to say 'hee haw' three times.

Cheat *

Number: 3 or more (more fun with 4 upwards)   *Age:* 6 upwards
Time: 3–5 minutes (best played as fast as possible)
Adult supervision: explaining rules and umpiring on conflicting calls

Cheat is a marvellously exciting game, and one that everyone can enjoy especially if it is played at a good, fast pace, without long pauses between each move.

After being shuffled the whole pack is dealt to the players, one card at a time. Everyone examines their hands and the player to the left of the dealer places one of his or her cards face down on the table and names its value at the same time. The value given need not be the card's real value; it may be, but it does not have to be – it's all part of the skill of the game. The next player to the left follows by placing one of his or her cards face down on the first one, and again gives a value   but this has to be the next *value above the first one called.* Again there is no obligation to give the card's real value, it's all a question of cheating convincingly, because the object of the game is to get rid of all one's cards before the other players get rid of theirs!

The game continues like this, with players placing cards on top of the growing pile in the centre, and calling the next highest value each time. At no time should any player let the others see the real value of the card he or she is playing.

At any time in the game, after a card has been played, players may challenge the identity of the card. Supposing that David has just played a card and called 'Six', Mary can challenge him and turn the card over to see what it really is. Now if David was cheating, and really played a card with a different value, he has to take all the cards in the central pile and add them to his hand! But if he did in fact play a 'six', then Mary's challenge was unfounded and she has to add all the cards in the centre to her hand! It's quite likely that as the game hots up, there may be several players all calling 'Cheat' at the same time; this is where the umpire comes in to decide who will be the challenger. (Another way of deciding this is to allow the player nearest the left-hand side of the player being challenged to become the challenger.) Whatever you decide, the cards in the centre have to be taken by one of the two, and the game resumes with the player to the left of the one challenged playing a card and announcing a value.

Play continues until one player succeeds in getting rid of all of his or her cards. That player is the winner.

Rolling Stone *

Number: 4, 5, or 6   *Age:* 7 upwards   *Time:* 5–10 minutes
Adult supervision: only to explain the rules

Before the game begins, a certain number of cards must be removed depending on the number of players:

If there are four players, remove all 2s, 3s, 4s, 5s, and 6s
If there are five players, remove all 2s, 3s, and 4s
If there are six players, remove all 2s

The players cut the cards to decide who will deal (aces count high), and the dealer deals the cards in a clockwise direction, one at a time and face down. When the dealing is complete, the players look at their cards and divide them into suits.

The player to the dealer's left selects a card from his or her hand and places this face up in the centre of the table. It's then up to the other players to play a card of the same suit, each aiming to be the first to get rid of all his or her cards. If all the players manage to play a card of the same suit, these are taken to one side and stay out of play for the rest of the game. The next 'trick' (set of cards) is started by the player who played the card with the highest value (aces high) in the last round.

Any player unable to play a card of the right suit is forced to pick up the cards already played in that trick and add them to his or her own hand. He or she then has to play the first card of the next trick, though none of the cards just picked up may be used for this. The player to use up all his or her cards wins the game.

Round the Corner *

Number: 3 or more   *Age:* 7 upwards   *Time:* 3–5 minutes
Adult supervision: only to explain rules
(Equipment: 20 counters each)

This game is very easy to learn and great fun to play. Each player is given 20 counters and all the cards are dealt out face down, one at a time, to all the players.

Play begins with the player to the left of the dealer who chooses one of his or her cards and places this face up in the centre of the table. The next player to the left looks at his or her cards to see if there is one which is the next in sequence, that is to say one that belongs to the same suit and one that is next in the numerical order: ace, 2, 3, 4, 5, 6, 7, 8, 9, 10, jack, queen, king. If the last card played happened to be a king, the next card in sequence is then an ace. This is known as a 'round the corner sequence', giving the game its name.

If the player does have the next card in sequence, this is played face up on the pile in the centre. If not, one of the counters is placed in the centre. The next player then either plays a card in sequence or puts a counter in the centre. When the last card of a suit has been played, the player who played it has an extra turn and can play any card he or she likes.

The first player to get rid of all his or her cards wins the round and takes all the counters from the centre. The other players must also pay the winner one counter for every card left in their hands. After an agreed number of rounds, the player with the most counters wins the game.

My Ship Sails *

Number: 4–7   *Age:* 6 upwards   *Time:* 3–5 minutes
Adult supervision: only to explain rules

The aim of the game is to collect seven cards of the same suit and cry 'My Ship Sails!' before any of the other players can do this; seven diamonds, seven spades, seven hearts, seven clubs – any of these can win the game.

The game begins with seven cards being dealt to each player. Any cards left over are set aside and are not used in the game. The players then look at their cards, and each chooses one he or she does not want to keep. These are placed face down on the table and are passed to the left. The players now pick up the cards passed to them from the right, and place them in their hands.

The game continues like this with players passing and collecting cards, until one player manages to collect seven cards of the same suit and calls triumphantly 'My Ship Sails!', laying his or her cards face upwards on the table. This player wins the game.

Go Boom *

Number: 2 or more   *Age:* 6 upwards   *Time:* 5 minutes
Adult supervision: only to explain rules

One player is chosen to be the dealer, and he or she deals out the cards face down, one at a time to each player, having first shuffled the pack. Each player is dealt seven cards altogether. The rest of the cards are placed face down on the table in a neat pile known as the stock.

Play begins with the player to the left of the dealer playing one of his or her cards and laying it face up beside the stock pile. The next player to the left does the same, and play continues like this moving to the left, providing that each player can play a card of the same suit as the first card or, failing that, of the same value. If the first card was a three of diamonds, for example, that would have to be followed by another diamond or another three.

Any player who has neither of the right cards must take a card from the top of the stock, and must carry on doing so in turn until he or she comes across a card that will match the first card. If all the cards in the stock have been used, the player says 'Pass' and the next player has a turn.

When every player has either played a card or passed, the round ends, and the player who played the highest value card (aces counting high) begins the next round. If two players played high cards of the same value, the first to play the card starts the next round.

The winner is the first player to get rid of all of his or her cards, an action which is usually accompanied with a shout of 'Boom!', bellowed as loudly as possible!

Beggar My Neighbour *

Number: 2–6   *Age:* 5 upwards   *Time:* 3–5 minutes   *Adult supervision:* only to explain rules and see they are followed

The cards are dealt out one at a time to each of the players and must be left face down. When all the cards have been dealt, the players form their hands into neat piles but still don't look at them.

Play starts with the player to the left of the dealer who turns over the top card of his or her pile and places it face up in the middle of the table. The others follow by playing in the same way.

Whenever a player turns up an ace or one of the three court cards, the next player must 'pay' a certain number of cards to the central pile. If a jack is turned up, one card is paid; if a queen is turned up, two cards are paid; if a king is turned up, three cards are played; and if an ace is turned up, four cards are played. However, if during the payment the player turns up an ace or a court card, the payment stops and the player to his or her left has to start paying the appropriate number of cards to him or her. This process continues round the group until one player makes a full payment *without* turning up an ace or court card and so wins the pile in the centre, which are added to the bottom of his or her pile.

The game continues with the last player playing his or her top card to the centre of the table. Players who have no cards left in front of them have to drop out, and the last player left in the game wins.

War *

Number: 2   *Age:* 5 upwards   *Time:* 3–5 minutes
Adult supervision: only to explain rules

In this easy game both players aim to be the one to win all his or her opponent's cards.

One of them deals the pack face downwards, one card at a time, until all the cards have been dealt. Each player arranges his or her cards in a neat pile, still face downwards. Play begins with both players lifting the top cards from their piles and placing them face up, side by side in the centre of the table. If one player plays a card with a higher value than the other player, he or she takes both cards. If the two cards are the same value, both players now play their next cards *face downwards* and then play the next card face up. Again if one of those is higher in value, the player who played it takes all the cards in the centre. If two cards of the same value are again played, the procedure is as before, with the next cards being played face downwards and the ones after them being played face up. This carries on until one player plays a card with a higher value.

The game continues like this until one player wins all the cards and defeats his or her opponent.

Rummy *

Number: 2–6   *Age:* 8 upwards   *Time:* 10 minutes   *Adult supervision:* only to explain rules and maybe play a hand

This is one of the most popular family card games which has been enjoyed by players of all ages for generations.

The game begins with the players deciding who will be dealer. They do this by each drawing a card from the pack. The dealer picks up the pack and deals cards to each of the players according to how many are playing:

> If 2 players play, they get 10 cards each.
> If 3 or 4 players play, they get 7 cards each.
> If 5 or 6 players play, they get 6 cards each.

The cards are dealt one at a time and face down. The remainder of the pack is placed in the middle of the table as the stock, and the top card from this is turned up and placed beside it to start the discard pile. The game is now set for play to begin.

Each of the players keeps his or her cards hidden from view by the others. They all study their cards, bearing in mind the object of the game which is to be the first to get rid of all the cards. Cards are disposed of by forming them into two types of sets and the process by which this is done is known as *melding*. Cards may either be melded groups or sequences. A group consists of three or more cards of the same value – three jacks, three fours, three twos, for instance. A sequence is formed from three or more consecutive cards of the same suit, which might be the ace, two, three and four of hearts (in Rummy the ace is a low-scoring card, so sequences of jack, queen, king and ace are not allowed).

Play begins with the player on the left of the dealer. He or she takes the top card from either the stock or the discard pile and adds it to his or her own hand. Any melds formed in the hand are then laid on the table face upwards and the first player ends his or her first play by discarding one card to the discard pile. The next player repeats the procedure of picking up one card and putting down any melds formed. Once a player has put down a meld, he or she may also add a card to any melds formed by other players, provided that card extends the meld. This process is called *laying-off*. Each player proceeds like this, picking up a card, laying down any melds, laying-off any cards and finally discarding a card. The first player to get rid of all of his or her cards wins the hand, and is awarded a score calculated from the cards held by the other players. Each card carries its pip value and court cards carry 10.

Any player who manages to get rid of all his or her cards in one turn is said to 'go rummy', which has the added advantage of doubling the score for that hand!

Play continues until one player reaches whatever figure was agreed on by the players before the game began.

BOARD GAMES

Nine Men's Morris *

Number: 2   *Age:* 8 upwards   *Time:* 5–10 minutes   *Adult supervision:* only to explain rules   (*Equipment:* a board and 18 counters)

This is one of the oldest surviving board games, having been a favourite pastime in ancient Egypt, Priam's Troy, first century AD Ceylon and Dark Age Scandinavia.

The game falls into two stages. In the first the counters are put on the board, in the second they are removed. In both cases careful strategy is involved to enable you to take your opponent's counters without losing too many of your own.

A board for *Nine Men's Morris* looks like this:

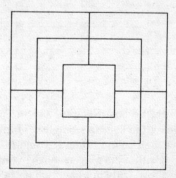

The players have nine counters each and they take it in turns to place a counter on any vacant point they choose, with the object of getting three counters in a row on any of the lines on the board. This process is called forming a 'mill'. Every time a mill is formed, that player is allowed to remove one of the opposing counters – but not one which forms a mill unless there are none others available. Having been removed, a counter stays out of play for the rest of the game.

Once the first stage is completed, the second stage begins, with the players moving one counter at a time along a line to any adjacent empty point. The aim in this stage is to form mills too. Players may break mills of their own by moving a counter from one and then moving it back again in the next turn. The advantage of this is that when any mills are formed (whether for the first time or as a re-formation), the player forming the mill may remove one of the opponent's counters.

The game ends when one player has only two counters left, or when the counters are so blocked that they cannot be moved.

Achi *

Number: 2   *Age:* 6 upwards   *Time:* 3–5 minutes   *Adult supervision:* only to explain rules   (*Equipment:* board and four counters per player)

Achi is a very popular West African board game, especially in Ghana. An *Achi* board looks like this:

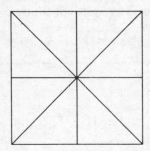

Play begins with the board empty, and the first eight moves are taken up with placing the counters on eight of the nine points on the board. Players place their counters one at a time, taking it in turns. Once the counters are in position the players move in turn, trying to get three of their counters in a row. Only one counter may be moved at a time and this must be moved along a line to a vacant point. No opposing counters are captured in *Achi*, the winner is the first player to get three counters in a row.

Nine Holes *

Number: 2   *Age:* 6 upwards   *Time:* 3–5 minutes   *Adult supervision:* only to explain rules   (*Equipment:* board and three counters per player)

You can still find *Nine Holes* boards scratched in cloister pavements of medieval cathedrals, where choirboys and priests enjoyed the game in their off-duty moments. Further afield the game was played by Arabs in Spain and even in temples in far-off Japan.

A *Nine Holes* board looks like this:

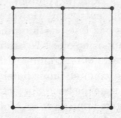

The game begins with the players placing their counters on the board one at a time. This takes up the first six moves. When they are all on the board, each player moves one counter to an adjacent, unoccupied point, moving along one of the lines. The object is to be the first to get three counters in a row. The player who achieves this wins the game.

Four Field Kono *

Number: 2   *Age:* 6 upwards   *Time:* 3–5 minutes   *Adult supervision:* only to explain rules   (*Equipment:* board and eight counters per player)

At the start of this popular Korean game all eight counters are on the board as shown. As in *Draughts*, and several other games included here, the object is to capture all one's opponent's pieces, or to block them so they cannot be moved.

The board for *Four Field Kono* looks like this:

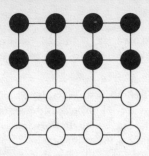

Players take it in turns to move, and each moves one counter at a time. When not making a capture, counters can only move along the lines one step to an adjacent point. However, unlike many similar games, capturing in this one involves jumping over one of *your own* counters, not one of the opposing ones! To capture an opposing counter, a counter has to jump over another counter of the same colour and land directly on the opposing counter immediately beyond. The captured counter is then removed from the board. In fact, at no time in *Four Field Kono* do opposing counters jump over each other.

The first player to capture or block all the opposing counters wins the game.

Gobang *

Number: 2   *Age:* 8 upwards   *Time:* 10 minutes or more   *Adult supervision:* only to explain rules   (*Equipment:* board and 100 counters per player)

Gobang is really a Japanese form of *Nine Holes*, though at first you might be forgiven for not recognizing it as such. In this game each player has 100 counters and they play on a board with no fewer than 324 squares! The board is simply a grid of squares 18 by 18, which can easily be drawn on a large piece of card or paper.

The players take it in turns to place their counters on the board, with the object of getting five counters in a row either vertically, horizontally or diagonally.

If both players are going so well that all 200 counters appear on the board without either of them forming a five-counter row, they start moving one counter at a time to a neighbouring empty square lying vertically or horizontally. You can't move counters diagonally in *Gobang*.

The first player to position five counters in a row wins.

Chess *

Number: 2   *Age:* 8 upwards   *Time:* seldom less than 10 minutes and often several hours (one championship match lasted 24½ hours)   *Adult supervision:* to explain rules, give a few practice games, and learn to be beaten with a good grace! (*Equipment:* chess-board and chess pieces)

Chess is one of the world's oldest and most fascinating games. First accounts place it in India during the eighth century, from where it spread westwards through Persia and Arabia to Europe. The game as played today probably came into being during the sixteenth century.

The game is played on a board with sixty-four squares, alternately black and white. The players sit opposite each other and the board is positioned so that each player has a white square at the lower right-hand corner. Each player has sixteen pieces, called 'men' – one set white, the other black.

At the beginning of the game the pieces are set out on the board like this:

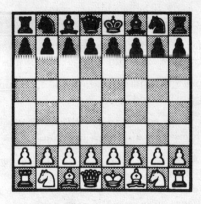

Each set of pieces consists of:

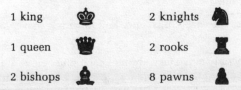

1 king	2 knights
1 queen	2 rooks
2 bishops	8 pawns

Note that the white queen always starts the game on a white square, and the black queen on a black square.

The rows on the chess-board have special names, which it's as well to learn before you start playing. The horizontal rows are called *ranks*, the vertical ones are known as *files*, and the diagonal ones are known as *diagonals*.

To decide who will start, one player holds out a black pawn in one fist and a white pawn in the other, and asks his opponent to choose one. The player who gets the white pawn always starts the game and uses the white set to play.

The players take it in turns to move one piece at a time. Opposing pieces may be captured simply by occupying the squares on which they are standing. The only piece on each side that cannot be captured is the king. But this can be threatened with being captured by being placed in a position known as 'check'. A king in check must be rescued from this state before any other move can be made. If the king cannot escape from check, however, the situation is called 'checkmate' and the king's player loses the game.

Each player on the board has a specific type of movement, as follows:

The *rooks* can move any distance along the ranks or files until their path is blocked. They can never move along the diagonals.

The *bishops* can move any distance along diagonals until their path is blocked. They can never move along the ranks or files.

The *queen* can move any distance in a straight line along ranks, files or diagonals until she is blocked.

The *king* can move one square in any direction. However, he is not allowed to move himself into a check position.

The *knights* must move in an L-shape, two squares along a rank or file and then to an adjoining square, either right or left, or up or down. In making their moves, the knights may jump over other pieces. They are the only men allowed to jump over other chess pieces like this. (The only other jumping that is allowed is the move known as *castling*, which is explained later on.)

Rooks, bishops, queens, kings and knights may move forwards or backwards.

The *pawns* may only move forward and each must move along its own file except when it captures an enemy piece, in which case it may move one square forward on a diagonal. Pawns may move two squares on their first move, but only one square in each move after that. If a pawn moves two squares on its initial move, and there is an enemy pawn on an adjacent file which could have captured it had it moved only one square, then it can be captured exactly as if it had only moved one square – the capturing pawn moves one square diagonally forward and the captured pawn is removed from the board. The en *passant* capture, if it is to be made, must be made *immediately* after the opposing pawn has made its two-square move. When a pawn reaches the eighth rank it is 'promoted' and becomes a queen, rook, bishop or knight, whichever the player chooses.

All the pieces except pawns capture in the same way. If an opposing piece stands on a square that can be reached by a king, a queen, rook, bishop or knight, the appropriate piece moves to that square and captures it. The captured piece is then removed from the board.

Pawns capture pieces in a different way. They cannot capture opposing pieces in the same file. They can only capture those that are diagonally one square ahead.

Both players are allowed one special move during the game. This move may be made only once and involves moving two pieces at once: the king and one rook. This is the 'jumping' move mentioned earlier, known as 'castling'. The move may be made only if:

(a) both king and rook are in their original positions and neither has already been moved,
(b) if the squares between the king and rook are empty,
(c) if the king is not in check, and
(d) if the two squares the king must cross are not guarded by opposing pieces. Castling consists of moving the king two squares towards the rook and then placing the rook on the square just jumped over by the king.

Castling has two main purposes – to move the king into a more secure position behind unmoved pawns, and to bring the two rooks closer together towards the centre of the board so that they are in a good position for a dramatic forward attack.

If a pawn reaches the far side of the board, it must be removed and can be replaced by a queen, rook, bishop or knight. Most players opt for a queen because she is the most flexible and useful piece on the board – not that it is very likely that there will be a game with more than two queens on the board. Just occasionally there are, though, and sometimes there have been as many as five in play at the same time!

Once a player touches a man it must be moved, and if it can't be moved the king must be moved instead, although the king cannot be moved by castling. Once a man has been moved and set down, the move is over and it's too late for second thoughts!

The aim of the game, as mentioned earlier, is to move into a position to capture the opposing king through checkmate, at which point a player warns his or her opponent by announcing 'Check!'. This is not obligatory, but it is customary to say it. When the opposing king is in no position to move at all, the player announces 'Checkmate!'

If a player isn't told that he or she is in check and makes a move that does not relieve the king, that move has to be taken back and the king has to be rescued first from the check position.

Not every game of chess ends with checkmate. Many players resign before the game gets to that stage because they realize their opponent is in a much stronger position. Other games end in draws in which neither player has the upper hand. There are half a dozen different reasons for ending a game of chess in a draw. They are:

Lack of force. This is when the pieces on the board are too weak to force a checkmate on either king.

Perpetual check. This happens when one player can go on and on checking the opposite king without ever being able to force a checkmate.

Stalemate. This happens when the next player to move cannot make a legal move according to the rules, but his king is not actually in check.

Repetition. This is when the same positions of all the pieces, both white and black, occur three times in the same game, with the same player being about to move each time. When this happens for the third time, the player whose turn it is can claim a draw.

The fifty moves rule. Either of the players can claim a draw if, during fifty moves by one of the players, no pawn has been moved and no pieces have been captured – unless the opponent can demonstrate that he or she could definitely win.

By agreement. If they want to, the players can agree to draw, though in a tournament game they are not allowed to do this before the thirtieth turn.

This is only a skeleton of one of the world's most intriguing and complex games. Most libraries stock several books on the strategy of chess, and there is no shortage of advice on the way to play. That said, you can enjoy playing chess and learn to play well just through getting a lot of practice. Once you know the rules and get used to the various moves, you can enjoy games at a simple level, developing your game as you improve.

Horseshoe *

Number: 2   *Age:* 5 upwards   *Time:* 3–5 minutes   *Adult supervision:* only to explain rules   (*Equipment:* board and two counters per player)

Horseshoe is one of those games that crops up all over the world under all sorts of local names, like the one by which it is known in China, *Pong Hau K'i*. It is a simple game which can be played with great enjoyment by young as well as old. A *Horseshoe* board is a simple five point pattern like this:

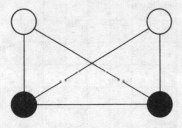

Each player has two counters which are placed on the four corners of the board as shown in the diagram. A coin is tossed to decide who starts, and the players take it in turns to move, with the first player sliding one of his or her counters down the line to the point in the centre. The second player must now slide a counter to the point that has just been vacated. Play continues like this, with one player moving one counter at a time, with the object of blocking the opposing counters, so that neither of them can be moved on the opponent's next turn to play.

Grasshopper *

Number: 2   *Age:* 6 upwards   *Time:* 3–5 minutes   *Adult supervision:* only to explain rules   (*Equipment:* board and ten counters per player)

Grasshopper is a game which can be played with the same board and same counters as *Draughts*. In this case each player has only ten counters and they are lined up in opposing corners.

The players take it in turns to move one counter at a time with the object of getting all of their counters into the opposing corner. To do this they may move counters in any direction to an adjacent, empty square.

They can also jump over counters of either colour, provided that the square beyond is empty, and as in *Draughts* it is possible for a player in one move to jump over several counters in succession, always providing that his counter lands each time on a vacant square. Unlike *Draughts* no counters are captured in *Grasshopper* and none are moved from the board. At the start of a game the board looks like this:

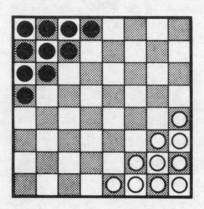

Madelinette *

Number: 2 *Age:* 5 upwards *Time:* 3–5 minutes *Adult supervision:* only to explain rules (*Equipment:* board and three counters per player)

This is a slightly more challenging form of *Horseshoe*, with an extra counter per player and a board with seven points.

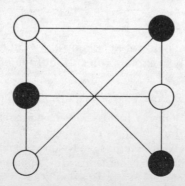

The game begins with the counters positioned as indicated. The first player begins by sliding one of his counters down a line to the vacant centre point. The second player now slides one of his counters to the newly vacated point. Play continues like this with both players moving one counter at a time to a vacant point on the board, always trying to position their counters in such a way that the opponent's counters are blocked and cannot be moved to the vacant point.

Draughts *

Number: 2   *Age:* 6 upwards   *Time:* 5–10 minutes   *Adult supervision:* only to explain rules   (*Equipment:* board and twelve counters per player)

The game of *Draughts* as we know it probably appeared in France at the beginning of the twelfth century, when someone had the bright idea of playing *Alquerque* (see elsewhere) on a chessboard. At the start of the game the counters are positioned as shown. Black moves first, and the players play alternately with the final objective of capturing all the other player's counters or blocking them in such a way that he or she cannot make any further moves.

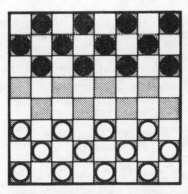

Only the black squares are used in the game, which means that all moves are made diagonally. Counters move one square at a time, unless they are capturing when they jump over an opposing counter to land on the square beyond. In every case a counter may only move to a vacant square. In the early part of the game, counters may only move forwards, towards the opponent. Once a counter has reached the far end of the board, it becomes a 'king' and it is usually distinguished from the other counters by being 'crowned' with another counter sitting on top of it. Thereafter it may move either forwards or backwards.

If a counter is in a position in which it can make a capture, it must do so. If any pieces that could have been captured are left uncaptured, the opponent may 'huff' the counter that missed the capture, and remove it from the game as a forfeit. So all possible captures must be made. However, if a counter has the option to make more than one capture at the start of a move, the player may select which one he wishes to take. (As an alternative to 'huffing', an opponent may insist that a player takes back his last move and replays it with the correct capturing move. So opponents have to be on the look-out as sharply as those capturing their pieces.)

The first player to capture all the opposing counters, or to block them so that they can no longer move, wins the game.

Mu-Torere *

Number: 2   *Age:* 7 upwards   *Time:* 3–5 minutes   *Adult supervision:* only to explain rules   *(Equipment:* board and four counters per player)

Mu-Torere is a Maori game from New Zealand, and in fact it is the only known board game of Maori origin. The board is shaped like an eight-pointed star with a circle in the middle, and each player has four counters. The central circle is called the 'putahi' and the points are called 'kewai'.

The game begins with the eight counters arranged on the kewai as shown. The player with the black counters moves first and the players then take it in turns, moving one counter at a time. The object of the game is to block an opponent's counters so that none of them can be moved.

Counters are moved from point to point subject to these conditions:

(a) The points must be unoccupied.
(b) Counters may be moved from a kewai to the putahi only if there are opposing counters on the kewais on either side.
(c) Counters may be moved from the putahi to the kewai or from one kewai to the adjacent kewai.

The first player to block his or her opponent's counters is the winner.

Reversi *

Number: 2   Age: 8 upwards   Time: 10 minutes or more
Adult supervision: only to explain rules
(Equipment: chessboard and sixty-four counters)

To play Reversi you will need a chessboard and sixty-four counters that are black on one side and white on the other. The counters are divided equally between the two players, and a coin or counter is tossed to see who will begin.

Black always plays first and begins by placing one counter black-side-up on one of the four squares in the centre of the empty board. White follows by placing a counter on another of the four central squares. From now on, the players take it in turns to place a counter on the board, and in the first four moves they fill the four central squares on the board. After this each move must be a taking move. If a player cannot make a taking move, he has to pass until he can do so.

A taking move consists of a player trapping one or more enemy pieces between two of his own. To do this a piece must be placed on the board next to an enemy piece and it must trap one or more enemy pieces between itself and another of the player's own pieces in a straight line – horizontally, vertically or diagonally – with no empty spaces in between. It is often possible in one move to take several pieces in different lines simultaneously.

Pieces that are taken are turned over to display the colour of the player that took them. Thus pieces once played are never removed from the board or moved from their original squares, but they may be turned over to transfer ownership several times in the course of the game.

The game ends when all sixty-four pieces have been played or when neither player can move. The winner is the player with the greater number of pieces of his colour on the board at the end of the game.

Alquerque *

Number: 2   *Age:* 7 upwards   *Time:* 5–10 minutes   *Adult supervision:* only to explain rules   (*Equipment:* board and 12 counters per player)

Alquerque arrived in Europe in the tenth century, when invading Arab armies took a break from conquests in Spain and sat down for a game. In many respects the game is similar to draughts, and draughts as we know it probably developed directly from *Alquerque*.

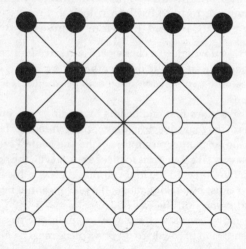

The game starts with each player's twelve counters arranged on the board as shown. Moves follow alternately with players moving counters along any of the lines to an adjacent point that is unoccupied. If a point is occupied but the one beyond it is vacant, then the player moving may jump over that counter to the vacant point. In so doing, the opposing counter is captured and removed from the board. Having done this the player may then move on to capture more opposing counters, even if it is necessary to change direction to do so.

In fact, any counter in a position to capture an opposing counter, must do so. If it doesn't, the other player may 'huff' the counter, removing it from the board as a forfeit.

Players may not jump over their own counters, nor are they allowed to 'pass'; they must make a move every go. The first player to remove all his opponent's counters wins the game.

Fox and Geese *

Number: 2   *Age:* 7 upwards   *Time:* 5–10 minutes   *Adult supervision:* only to explain rules   (*Equipment:* board and 14 counters (1 white, the rest black))

This is an old Scandinavian game, old enough to have been enjoyed by the Vikings back in the Dark Ages. It is something of a curiosity among board games in that the players have a totally different number of counters; one has thirteen black counters, representing the geese, the other has just one white one, the fox.

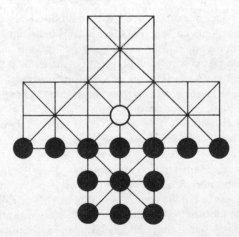

Play starts with the counters positioned on the board as shown. The fox moves first, the player with the geese follows, and moves alternate like this throughout the game. The objective as far as the fox is concerned is to capture enough geese to prevent them from trapping him. From the point of view of the geese, they win the game if they trap the fox in a way that prevents him from moving.

Both the fox and the geese can move along any of the lines to a neighbouring point, provided that it is vacant. The fox can capture geese by jumping over them on to a vacant point beyond, but the geese can neither jump over the fox, nor over each other.

If the geese crowd the fox into a corner, so that he cannot move, they win the game. If the fox captures enough geese to prevent them doing this he wins.

GAMES WITH BITS AND PIECES

Spangy *

Number: 5   *Age:* 5 upwards   *Time:* 3–5 minutes   *Adult supervision:* only to explain rules and see they are followed
(*Equipment:* selection of marbles per player)

Spangy is a popular game played with marbles. The players mark a square on the ground, and each places a marble in the square to form the following pattern: one marble at each corner and one in the centre.

Then taking it in turns, each player shoots a marble at the ones in the square. (There are various ways of shooting marbles but one of the commonest is to 'knuckle' the marble. This is done by placing the back of the shooting hand on the ground, with the knuckle of the forefinger touching the ground too. The marble rests on the forefinger, and the thumb is put behind the forefinger and then flicked out sharply to shoot the marble.)

Marbles are usually shot about 10 metres (33 feet) from the square – but players can stand closer to make it easier. A player may claim any marble he knocks out of the square, and if one of his marbles stops close enough to one for him to flick the two together, by using the forefinger and thumb of one hand, that can be claimed too. (Winning marbles in this way is called 'spanning'.)

Each player picks up his shooting marble at the end of his turn.

Bounce Eye *

Number: 2   *Age:* 5 upwards   *Time:* 2–3 minutes   *Adult supervision:* only to explain rules and see they are followed
(*Equipment:* a selection of marbles per player

Unlike many marbles games, this one involves players dropping their marbles instead of shooting them. The players begin by marking a target circle of about 30 cm (12 inches) in diameter on the ground. They then toss a coin to see who will start, each having first placed one or more marbles in a group inside the circle.

Each player in turn stands over the circle and drops a marble on to those below. A player who knocks any of the marbles out of the circle wins them, but has to add an extra marble if none are knocked out. The game continues until all the marbles have been knocked out of the circle and claimed by one or other of the players.

Ring Taw *

Number: any small number   *Age:* 5 upwards   *Time:* 3–5 minutes   *Adult supervision:* only to explain rules and see they are followed   (*Equipment:* a selection of marbles per player)

Ring Taw is a very popular marbles game which uses the other common name for a marble in its own game – *taw*. A *taw* is the name sometimes given to a marble that is actually being shot in a game, as opposed to one that is being shot at.

The game begins with two circles being drawn on the ground. The larger has a diameter of about 6.3 metres (7 feet), and the inner one has a diameter of about 30 centimetres (12 inches). At the beginning of the game, each player puts one or two marbles inside the inner circle. Each one then takes a turn in shooting from outside the outer circle.

Any player who knocks one or more marbles from the inner circle is allowed to keep them, and can have another shot from wherever the marble he first shot came to rest. Anyone who fails to knock a marble out of the inner circle has to leave his shooting marble where it stopped because his turn has ended. From then on the players may shoot at any marbles inside either of the circles. A player whose shooting marble is hit must pay a marble to the player who hit it. After the first round, every player shoots from wherever his shooting marble came to rest. The game ends when all the marbles have been knocked out of the inner circle.

Dice Shot *

Number: any number   *Age:* 5 upwards   *Time:* 3–5 minutes
Adult supervision: only to explain rules and see they are
followed   (*Equipment:* one dice, one filed marble and a
selection of marbles per player)

In this marbles game the target is rather unusual. Instead of shooting at
ordinary marbles, the players shoot instead at a dice balanced on top of a
marble that has been filed down on two sides to make it slightly more
stable.

The game is divided into rounds for each of which one player in turn
becomes the *dice-keeper*, which means that he receives one marble from
each of the other players before he shoots. If a player succeeds in
knocking the dice off the filed marble, the dice-keeper must pay that
player the number of marbles shown on the upper face of the dice. If the
player misses, the dice-keeper keeps the marbles.

The game continues until everyone has had a turn as dice-keeper.

Beetle *

Number: 2–6   *Age:* 6 upwards   *Time:* 10 minutes   *Adult
supervision:* only to explain rules   (*Equipment:* one dice; a
sheet of paper and pencil for each player)

Beetle is a popular family game that's great fun to play and great fun to
watch.

The object of the game is to be the first to draw a beetle, but this can
only be done after the correct values have been thrown on the dice. The
beetle has thirteen parts: a body, a head, a tail, two eyes, two feelers and
six legs. No part can be drawn until its correct value has been thrown,
and the values for the body and head must be thrown before other parts
can be attached to them, which stands to reason.

A completed beetle should look something like this:

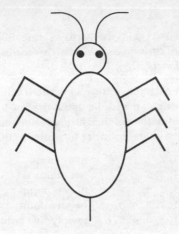

You can play with a special beetle dice, which has faces marked for the various parts of the beetle's body, but an ordinary dice serves just as well if you give these values to the various parts:

1 for the body
2 for the head
3 for each leg
4 for each eye
5 for each feeler
6 for the tail

The players throw the dice once in each turn, and each must throw a 1 (for the body) before he can start drawing. Once the body has been drawn, the head, legs and tail can be added, but the eyes and feelers can only be added after a 2 has been thrown and the head drawn in.

The game can be played for points, too, with each round coming to an end when one player completes a beetle. This player scores 13 points, and the others get 1 point for every part of their beetle that has been drawn. The first player to score 51 points wins the game.

Hearts *

Number: 2 or more   *Age:* 6 upwards   *Time:* 5–10 minutes
Adult supervision: only to explain rules   (*Equipment:* six
dice (or special *Hearts* dice))

Hearts begins with each player throwing the six dice. The player with
the highest total becomes the leader and is the first to throw in the game
proper. After throwing the six dice he studies them to see if one of the
following patterns is there, in order to work out the score:

1, 2	five points
1, 2, 3	ten points
1, 2, 3, 4	fifteen points
1, 2, 3, 4, 5	twenty points
1, 2, 3, 4, 5, 6	twenty-five points

If the player has thrown a double, only one of the dice counts, so a
throw of 1, 2, 3, 3, 4, 6 would score only ten points for the 1, 2, 3. Triples
are also ignored unless the player throws a triple 1. If this happens, the
player's whole score is removed and the player has to start scoring again
from the beginning!

Players keep a written note of their scores as the game progresses,
moving to the left from the dealer. The first player to reach 100 wins the
game.

Pig *

Number: 2 or more   *Age:* 6 upwards   *Time:* 3–5 minutes
Adult supervision: only to explain rules, and possibly help
keep the scores   (*Equipment:* one dice)

Although *Pig* is one of the easiest of dice games, it is exciting and
requires some daring because there is a one-in-six chance that an over-
eager player could lose his score.

The game begins with the players taking it in turns to throw the
dice. The one with the lowest number starts. (If several players throw the
same low number, they all throw again to see who has the lowest second
time round.) Each player must make a mental note of the number they
have thrown, to add to their score on the following rounds.

On the next round each player may throw the dice as many times in a go as he likes, adding the numbers shown on the dice to his score after each throw. However, if the player throws a 1, that wipes out any points scored in that turn; so it's a matter of daring. The longer a player carries on throwing, the higher his score climbs, but the risk of losing it through throwing a 1 gets higher too. Of course, a player can end a turn whenever he wants, keeping the points scored. When this happens the dice is passed to the next player on the left to have a turn. The first player to reach a score of 50 wins the game.

Round the Clock *

Number: 3 or 4   Age: 6 upwards   Time: 3–5 minutes   Adult supervision: only to explain rules   (Equipment: 2 dice; paper and pencil for scores (if necessary))

As its name suggests, Round the Clock is a game in which the players try to throw the dice to progress from 1 to 12 in sequence, the winner being the first player to do this.

The players take it in turns to throw the two dice, and examine the throws they have made. If a player throws a 1, for example, in his first throw, he has got off to a good start. (The value of the other dice can be ignored.) If he had already thrown a 1 in an earlier round and wanted a 3, however, and his other dice happened to show a 3, that could be used instead of the 1. So with the numbers from 1 to 6, players may use either of the values shown to suit their purposes. Of course, if the player with a 1 and 3 wanted a 4, he could add the two together to produce that. All that matters in the game is that the player should progress from 1 to 12 through each of the intervening numbers. Above 7, both dice will have to be used to produce the correct totals.

The player who reaches 12 first wins the game.

Chicago *

Number: 2 or more   *Age:* 6 upwards   *Time:* 5–10 minutes
Adult supervision: only to explain rules and check rounds
(*Equipment:* 2 dice, paper and pencil for rounds and scores)

This game is based on all the possible scoring combinations of the two dice, and has eleven rounds. In each of these rounds the players throw the dice once each, with the aim of throwing the correct combination for that particular round. At the end of the eleventh round the player with the highest score wins the game.

The only players who can score in each round are the ones who throw the correct totals, which correspond to the number of the round in which they are throwing. In the first round, for example, everyone will be hoping for a 2, the first and lowest combination of two dice. In the second they will be after a 3, in the third a 4, and so on. Every time a player manages to throw the right combination, that total is added to his score. If the wrong combination is thrown, no points are scored in that round.

After eleven rounds the scores are counted, and the player with the highest wins.

Fifty *

Number: 2 or more   *Age:* 6 upwards   *Time:* 3–5 minutes
Adult supervision: only to explain rules   (*Equipment:*
2 dice)

Fifty is an exciting, but simple, dice game in which the players race each other to be the first to reach a total of fifty.

The players take it in turns to throw the two dice, hoping that the pip values on them will be the same, because in *Fifty* this is the only way to score, with two 1s, two 2s, two 4s, two 5s and two 6s. In each case the doubles carry a score of 5 points, except for a double 6 which is worth 25 (throw two of these in a row and you win!), and double 3, which removes a player's whole score.

The first player to reach fifty wins the game.

Kayles ᴧ

Number: 2   *Age:* 5 upwards   *Time:* 3–5 minutes   *Adult supervision:* only to explain rules and take suitable safety precautions with matches   (*Equipment:* about 20 used matchsticks or cocktail sticks (though less would do))

Kayles was invented by the great British king of games and puzzles, H. E. Dudeney, who created many of today's most intriguing games and puzzles in the early part of this century.

In this game the matchsticks are arranged in a long line end to end, and the players remove either one or two matchsticks which are touching each other, with the object of being the player to pick up the last matchstick.

A few practice games will show that careful thought helps in this game, deciding how to manipulate the matchsticks your opponent can pick up, as well as deciding how many to pick up yourself in order to pick up the final one.

Another version of this game is the exact opposite. In this the rules are the same except that the player to pick up the last matchstick loses the game. It's best to decide which you intend to play before your game begins!

Nim *

Number: 2   *Age:* 6 upwards   *Time:* 3–5 minutes   *Adult supervision:* only to explain rules and take safety precautions with matches   (*Equipment:* 15 used matchsticks or cocktail sticks)

Like many deceptively simple games, *Nim* can prove to be a wonderful challenge between two players of equal ability. It's also a game which is very easy to learn and one that children will enjoy playing.

There are several variations of *Nim*, but the basic version, which is the oldest and probably originated in China, uses fifteen matchsticks arranged as follows: three matchsticks in the first row, five in the second and seven in the third.

Players take it in turns to play, and they may pick up any number of matchsticks from any one of the rows in each turn. So one player could remove all of the matchsticks from one row, or just one, but may not touch any of the matchsticks in the other rows. The object of the game is to pick up the last matchstick and so win.

An alternative form of *Nim* works in the opposite way. The player who forces his opponent to pick up the last matchstick wins the game.

Ends *

Number: 4   *Age:* 7 upwards   *Time:* 3–5 minutes
Adult supervision: only to explain rules   (*Equipment:* a set of dominoes)

The aim of *Ends* is to be the first player to get rid of all of your dominoes. Each player starts by drawing seven dominoes and the one with the double six lays this face upwards on the table. The next player on the left tries to add a matching domino to one end of the double six, and so play continues round the table. If a player finds that none of his dominoes has the right number of pips to match those at either end of the line, he has to ask the player on his left for a suitable one. If that player has one, he must give it to the player who asked for it. If not, the request passes to the next player and so on until one produces the right domino and gives it to the player who first asked for it. If it happens that the request goes right round the table and back to the player who asked for the domino in the first place, then he may play *any* domino in his hand at either end of the line, without it needing to match.

Play continues like this until one player gets rid of all of his dominoes.

Fours *

Number: 3, 4, or 5   *Age:* 7 upwards   *Time:* 5–10 minutes
Adult supervision: only to explain rules   (*Equipment:* a set of dominoes)

This is one of the simplest domino games, and is one that most players learn when they start playing.

After choosing a leader, each player draws a certain number of dominoes from the set, depending on how many are playing the game. If three are playing, each takes nine dominoes; if four are playing, each takes seven; and if four are playing, each takes five. The remaining dominoes are put to one side and are not used.

The object of the game is to be the first player to get rid of all the dominoes in your hand. Players play dominoes that match those at either end of the line and a player may carry on playing for as long as he or she can match dominoes (if you are very lucky, you may be able to get rid of all your dominoes in one go and so win the game). Normally most players will need to play two or more turns before getting rid of their hands. The first player to get rid of his dominoes wins, but occasionally the game gets blocked and no one can move. Whenever this happens, the players add up the number of pips on the dominoes they have left, and the player with lowest total is the winner.

Blocking *

Number: 2–4   *Age:* 6 upwards   *Times:* 3–5 minutes
Adult supervision: only to explain rules   (*Equipment:* a set of dominoes)

The dominoes are placed face downwards and are well shuffled. Each player draws seven dominoes. The rest are put to one side, and are not used in the game. The player with the highest individual domino plays first; if it is a double, he has an extra go. The next player lays down a domino with pips that match one end of the first domino. Play continues in this way with players matching pips at either end of the line of dominoes. If a player cannot play, he passes a turn. The game ends when one player lays down the last of his dominoes, or when no further play is possible, in which case the winner is the player with the lowest total left in his hand.

Blind Hughie *

Number: 2–5   *Age:* 6 upwards   *Time:* 3–5 minutes
Adult supervision: only to explain rules   (*Equipment:* a set of dominoes)

In this popular children's game the players draw a certain number of dominoes according to the number of players. When there are two or three players, each one draws seven dominoes; when there are four or five, each one draws five dominoes. Players may not look at the dominoes they have drawn; they have to remain face down on the table in a row.

The game begins with the lead player (chosen by lot) turning over the domino on the extreme left of his row and placing this in the middle of the table. In turn the others look at their left-hand dominoes and see if they can match them to either end of the line on the table. If they can, the dominoes are played. If they cannot, the dominoes are moved to the right-hand end of their rows, again placed face down.

Play continues round the players until one of them wins by playing all the dominoes in his hand, or until the game is blocked and no one can play. If this happens, no one wins.

GAMES TO PLAY AT SCHOOL

Playgroup Games
Classroom Games
Playground Games
Playing-Field Games

PLAYGROUP GAMES

Traffic Lights *

Number: any number   *Age:* 5 and under   *Time:* 3–5 minutes
Adult supervision: acting as leader

Traffic Lights is an energetic game that can be played either indoors or outside in fine weather, though if played inside it requires a large area like a hall or gym.

The leader stands at one end of the playing area with the children lined up at the other. The leader's back is turned to the children as he counts '1–2–3–4 Green Light!' On the words 'Green Light', the children must run towards the leader whose back is still turned and who is now counting '1–2–3–4 Red Light'. On the words 'Red Light', the children must stop in their tracks. The leader turns round suddenly to catch any children still running. Any caught have to go back to the far end of the playing area to start again.

The first child to reach the leader while the lights are green is the winner.

Hide and Seek

Number: any number   *Age:* 5 and under   *Time:* 5–10 minutes   *Adult supervision:* possibly to go in search of players hiding, otherwise to make sure no one can hide anywhere dangerous

Of all the time-honoured children's games, *Hide and Seek* is still one of the most popular and exciting. It can be played in two ways. In one form one child is given a minute to run away and hide before all the others set off like a pack of hounds to find him or her. In the other version all the children hide and the adult has to set off to look for them.

You can play *Hide and Seek* both indoors and out in the garden, in winter and in summer. You can even hide yourself and let the children try and find you – if you can think of a suitable place to hide, that is.

Button Bag (* optional)

Number: any number   *Age:* 5 and under   *Time:* 5–10 minutes
Adult supervision: providing materials, marking throwing
line and helping with counting   (*Equipment:* 10 buttons
and a large paper bag with a square base per player, a marker
for the throwing line)

This is a throwing and counting game in which the players can either compete against each other, or against themselves, trying to improve their score as they get more accurate.

The paper bags are opened up with the tops turned down and a weight placed in the bottom of each to prevent them falling over. These are lined up in a row on the floor with about 60 cms (24 inches) between them. The throwing line is marked the correct distance from the bags. This can be judged only according to the skill and age of the players, but wherever you decide to put it, mark the line with the strip of wood or material to show where the players must stand when they throw their buttons into the bags.

Each player stands in front of his or her bag and throws the ten buttons one after the other towards it. When all the buttons have been thrown, the players take out the ones in the bag, counting them aloud one by one. Next time they must try to improve on their score.

Bingo *

Number: any number   *Age:* 5 and under   *Time:* 3–5 minutes
Adult supervision: preparing game and helping with play
(*Equipment:* one Bingo card per player, several sets of small
squares of card numbered 1 to 10, bag)

Make one Bingo card for each player on a large sheet of paper or card and divide it into six squares numbered variously between 1 and 10. No two cards should be the same. Put all the individually numbered squares into the bag, give each child a Bingo card and you are ready to begin.

Pass the bag round the group, allowing the children to draw one number at a time. If the number drawn matches one on the card, the player keeps it and places it on the card (over the right square). If the number does not match one on the card, it must be returned to the bag. The first player to complete his or her card shouts 'Bingo!' and wins the game.

Across the Great Divide *

Number: any number   *Age:* 5 and under   *Time:* 3–5 minutes
Adult supervision: placing markers and judging jumps
(*Equipment:* 2 markers about a metre (3 feet) long, of wood,
rope or tape)

This is a jumping game in which the players take it in turns to jump over
a gap that slowly gets wider and wider. Start by placing the two markers
side by side with about 5 cms (2 inches) between them. All the players
line up on one side and jump the Great Divide one after the other. Now
increase the gap slightly and let them jump again. After everyone has
had a chance at jumping the gap, it is widened a little further until finally
it has reached a width that no one can jump. The last player to cross the
Great Divide successfully is the winner.

Name Chain

Number: any number   *Age:* 5 and under   *Time:* 3–5 minutes
Adult supervision: asking questions

Sit the players in a circle, and ask them a series of questions which they
must try to answer with words that all begin with the same letter. The
first question usually requires a first name as an answer; for example,
'What is your Daddy's name?' Even if the child just answers 'Daddy', that
will give the letter which must begin all the other answers:

> 'And what animals does Daddy like?'
> 'Dogs', or 'Donkeys' answers one child.
> 'What does Daddy open to leave a room?'
> 'Door' comes the answer from another, and so the questions
> and answers continue until the simple possibilities have been
> covered.

Move from one letter to another fairly quickly, encouraging the children
to think of familiar objects that begin with the same letter by asking
questions that guide them in those directions.

Teacher

Number: any number   *Age:* 5 and under   *Time:* 3–5 minutes
Adult supervision: only to explain the game and see that
everyone has a turn   (*Equipment:* a ball)

One of the children is chosen to be 'Teacher', and the others sit round
him in a circle. The teacher takes the ball and rolls it to one of the players
in the circle, having called out his or her name. The player whose name
has been called catches the ball and rolls it back to the Teacher. The
game progresses like this until every child has had a go at receiving and
returning the ball. Then the Teacher selects another player to take his
place and the game continues as before. Let everyone have a go at being
Teacher, and once the children get the hang of the game let them play it
as fast as they can.

Colour Dip *

Number: any number   *Age:* 5 and under   *Time:* 5–10 minutes
Adult supervision: preparing cards and monitoring game
(*Equipment:* an old pack of playing cards, brush and paints,
or coloured pens)

This game takes some time to prepare, but once ready the cards can be
used for similar games later.

Cover the face of the playing cards with the primary colours that a
child can easily learn, as well as some familiar ones like orange, black
and white. Avoid colours that are difficult to distinguish from each
other, or ones with unusual names.

Sit the players in a circle, shuffle the cards and deal five to each
player. The remaining cards are placed face down as a stack.

The players look at their cards, and the one to the left of the adult
dealer asks the player on the left for a colour. If the player has the card, he
must pass it. If not, he says 'Dip', and the player asking takes the top card
from the stack. If the card asked for is on the top, the player shows it and
gets another turn; if it isn't, the card stays in the hand. The object of the
game is to be the first to get four cards of the same colour, and the player
who does this is the winner.

Shopping

Number: any number   *Age:* 5 and under   *Time:* 15 minutes or
longer   *Adult supervision:* providing empty containers and
helping with the paper money   (*Equipment:* empty food
containers and packaging, paper and plastic money)

You'll need to gather a fair selection of empty cereal packets, margarine
boxes, yoghurt tubs, and any other type of food packaging that can be
hygenically cleaned and safely used for this game. Let the children help
you set up the shop, arranging the packages on the shelves and possibly
pricing them in a simple way that ties in with play money the
'customers' will be using.

 Two or three children can then work in the shop serving customers,
taking their money and helping to pack their bags – again a supply of
supermarket carrier bags is useful.

 The customers can make out simple shopping lists of things they
want to buy and can use their play money to pay for the goods. Keep the
pricing simple at this stage to avoid the need for too many complicated
sums in paying change. Let the customers take their goods 'home',
unpack them and then return them to the shop for another visit.

 The more goods available, the more fun the game will be, and if you
have the space add to them so that the game can be played time after
time.

Spot the Number

Number: any number   *Age:* 5 and under   *Time:* 5–10 minutes
Adult supervision: preparing cards and removing them
when the players have their eyes closed   (*Equipment:* 10 cards,
each marked with a number from 1 to 10)

The players sit in a circle with the cards spread out face upwards in the
middle. The adult sits with them and tells them to close their eyes at the
start of each round. While the eyes are closed, one or occasionally two of
the cards are removed and the players are told to open their eyes and
study the ones left behind.

 'Which card is missing?' asks the adult, and the children must say
which number has disappeared from the group. When this has been
found, they close their eyes again, the number is replaced and another
one is taken.

Obstacle Courses * (optional)

Number: any number   *Age:* 5 and under   *Time:* 10–15 minutes   *Adult supervision:* setting up course with children's help, making sure it is safe   (*Equipment:* large cardboard cartons, chairs, milk crates, large inner tubes (inflated and possibly hung from a tree), benches, or anything that could be used to construct an obstacle course)

Children of all ages love playing on obstacle courses, and if the space and facilities are available it is worth taking the trouble to construct one. The children will enjoy helping too. They may have ideas on where to position cartons through which they have to crawl, for example, or how to make a bridge between two milk crates with a firm plank. Variety rather than complexity should be the key feature of the obstacle course, and no part of it should be too difficult for any one child to tackle. Obviously check that everything is quite safe before the competitors start on the course.

Let the players take it in turns to go through the course, trying to go as fast as they can without knocking over any of the objects or treading on the ground when they are supposed to have their feet off it. If you want to make the game competitive, let the fastest and least destructive player be the winner. Perhaps he or she could arrange the next obstacle course

Mind Reading

Number: any number   *Age:* 5 and under   *Time:* 3–5 minutes
Adult supervision: answering questions

The players don't actually 'mind read' in this game, they just ask questions to try and find out what the adult is thinking of. Clearly the objects must be things or people well known to all the players, and the aim of the game is to encourage children to ask questions that will help them discover the answer.

They will almost certainly need help at first and this can be given in questions like, 'Wouldn't it be easier to know if I was thinking of a person or a thing?', or 'Do you think what I'm thinking of is in this room or outside? How would you ask that?'

Let the children ask as many questions as they like until it is clear that they are stuck. Then tell them the answer and explain how close they came to it. If one of them does come up with the right answer, let him or her think of the next topic.

Follow My Leader

Number: any number   *Age:* 5 and under   *Time:* 3–5 minutes
Adult supervision: leading very young children and seeing that
the older ones follow the leader in every movement

The object of this game is to get the players to watch the leader closely
and imitate everything that he or she does. In the case of very young
players (two- and three-year-olds), this will just be a matter of following
the leader round the room, out of one door and in through another, for
example. Players of four and five years of age will want something a little
more demanding, and they should be able to follow the leader in gesture
as well as direction. If the leader hops at one point or raises a hand, the
followers must do the same. There are no winners or losers in this game,
but if you notice a player who has forgotten to do something, or a leader
whose actions are too difficult to follow, give a gentle reminder.

Alphabet Angling

Number: any number   *Age:* 5 and under   *Time:* 5–10
minutes   *Adult supervision:* preparing letters and 'fishing
tackle', and helping with 'catch'   (*Equipment:* large squares of
paper each bearing one letter of the alphabet (make 1 alphabet
between three children), paper-clips, string, magnets and 'rods')

Each of the players is given a special fishing rod made from a pole to
which is tied a length of string with a horseshoe magnet at the other end.
The 'fish' are squares of paper, each with a letter of the alphabet, to which
a paper-clip has been attached.

The 'fish' are scattered across the floor, over a fairly wide area, and
the fishermen sit around the edge with the rods. One by one they may
each catch a fish and bring it to the 'bank'. Then they must hold up the
letter and say what it is. The letter becomes part of their catch and the
next player has a turn. Players who need help with the letters should be
encouraged to try and catch the same letter next time round to see if they
can remember its shape. When all the fish have been caught, shuffle
them and throw them back for another session.

CLASSROOM GAMES

Draughts-Board Observation *

Number: any number   *Age:* 7 upwards   *Time:* 3–5 minutes
Adult supervision: arranging board and judging answers
(*Equipment:* paper and pencil per player, and a draughts-board
with 8 black pieces and 8 white pieces)

In this observation game, the players must first draw a grid of 8 × 8
squares representing a draughts-board (if they are given graph paper,
this will make the job quicker). When everyone is ready, the draughts-
board with the pre-arranged pieces is revealed for ten seconds, during
which time the players have to try and memorize the position of the
pieces. Whon time is up the board Is hidden and the players fill in their
own grids, trying to remember the correct pattern of the pieces on the
board.

By varying the number of the pieces and using white ones as well as
black, this can be a challenging and stimulating game. After each round
the player whose grid is closest to the original lay-out scores a point. The
player with the highest score at the end of the game is the winner

Buried Words *

Number: any number   *Age:* 8 upwards   *Time:* 5 minutes
Adult supervision: preparing sentences and providing answers
(*Equipment:* paper and pencil per player)

Buried Words does take slightly longer to prepare than some word
games, but it is also more of a challenge for the players and is worth the
effort.

The game consists of the players being given a series of sentences in
which are hidden words. The words are buried, so to speak, among the
other words in the sentence. For example the word 'goat' is buried in this
sentence: 'You'll only catch the bus if you go at once.' ('. . . go at . . .'
gives 'goat').

All the players need be told is the topic covered by the words; in the case of 'goat', therefore, they would be finding the name of an animal. Any topic can be used, and the sentences can contain more than one buried word if this is practical.

The player with the highest number of discovered words at the end of the five minutes is the winner.

Synonyms *

Number: any number   *Age:* 8 upwards   *Time:* 5 minutes
Adult supervision: setting words and judging answers
(*Equipment:* paper and pencil per player, blackboard)

This game is an entertaining way of getting children to extend their vocabulary. A list of twenty words is written on the blackboard which the players must copy down on the left-hand side of their sheet of paper. On the word 'Go!' the players must try to think of synonyms (words with the same or similar meaning) for all the words. Some words may have more than one synonym, in which case the players can write down as many as they like. The player with the longest and most accurate list at the end of five minutes is the winner.

Colour Changes

Number: any large number   *Age:* 6 upwards   *Time:* 1–2 minutes   *Adult supervision:* giving colours to players and seeing that none of the others look while they are changing places

This is one of those deceptively simple games which is actually quite difficult to play well.

Six players stand in a straight line in front of the others. Each of the six is given a colour, perhaps 'Red, yellow, blue, purple, orange, white'. The other players are then told to turn away, so that they are unable to see the six 'colours'. The colours change places, and when they are re-arranged the players turn back to them and try to name them by colour. This isn't as easy as it may sound.

Ship Game *

Number: any number   *Age:* 8 upwards   *Time:* 3–5 minutes
Adult supervision: setting questions   (*Equipment:* paper and pencil per player)

You can play this word game in two ways. The players can either list as many words as they can that end with 'ship', or they can be given clues that lead them to the answers. In either case the aim of the game is to stretch their vocabulary.

In the first version the players should be given a set amount of time to list words like: worship, leadership, partnership, ownership, friendship and scholarship. The player with the longest list of words at the end of the period is the winner.

To play the game in the second way, the players need to be given clues to point them towards the 'ship' words. In the case of the examples above, these might be: 'Which ship commands others?' (answer: leadership), or 'Which ship is shared by somebody else?' (answer: partnership). Again, the player with the longest list of correct answers at the end of the time allowed is the winner.

Heights

Number: any number   *Age:* 5 upwards   *Time:* 2–3 minutes
Adult supervision: only to judge result

This is a silly game that always raises a lot of laughs. The players hold hands to form a circle, and on the word 'Go!' shut their eyes and start trying to arrange themselves in order of height from tallest down to shortest, moving round the circle as necessary until the right order is achieved. (Obviously they let go of each other's hands as they move, but they have to gauge their heights as best they can while holding hands.)

Conversations

Number: any number   *Age:* 6 upwards   *Time:* 3–5 minutes
Adult supervision: only to explain rules

Conversations is played in groups of about five or six players. Each group has a conversation in which each player in turn says one word as the conversation passes round the group. So the first player might say 'Today', the second might add 'I', the third might continue 'went', and so the conversation progresses, with as many cranky and funny ideas as possible to make the game fun.

What's Changed? *

Number: any number   *Age:* 6 upwards   *Time:* 3–5 minutes
Adult supervision: arranging and changing objects
(*Equipment:* a dozen articles that can be arranged easily on a table, paper and pencil per player)

The adult arranges the objects on a table in a definite and fairly simple formation, while the players are either out of the room or cannot see the arrangement taking place. When the objects are ready, the players have fifteen seconds to study them before they are hidden from sight. The adult then alters the position of some of the objects and lets the players have another look before they list the objects that have been moved.

The player with the most complete list is the winner and is allowed to arrange the objects in the next round.

The Dog and the Cat

Number: any number   *Age:* 7 upwards   *Time:* 2–3 minutes
Adult supervision: only to explain rules and provide 'dog' and 'cat'   (*Equipment:* two articles to represent 'dog' and 'cat' (a rubber and a pencil, for example))

Here's a silly game which can be great fun and will certainly keep the players well occupied. Start by sitting them in a circle. One player is chosen to be the leader, and is given the two objects representing the 'dog' and the 'cat'.

When everyone is ready the leader starts the game by passing the 'dog' to the player on the left, saying 'Here is the dog.' The player receiving the object asks, 'The what?' 'The dog' answers the leader. Now the second player passes the 'dog' to the next player on the left using the same rigmarole, 'Here is the dog.' 'The what?' asks the player again, but the second player does not answer the question. He or she passes it back to the leader who must answer 'The dog.'

Play continues in this way with the players all using the same words and the question 'The what?' always being passed back down the line to the leader. But the fun comes from the other direction, because as soon as the leader has passed the 'dog', he or she also passes the 'cat'. This is passed in just the same way to the leader's right, with the remark 'Here is the cat.' The 'cat' is passed from player to player to the right, with the question 'The what?' again being passed back down the line to the leader every time.

While both animals are passing down the lines on which they started, all should be well; but after they have crossed, chaos is likely to ensue with players mixing up the animals and getting confused as to who is asking questions about which.

When both the 'dog' and the 'cat' have found their way back to the leader, give someone else a chance to be leader for the next game.

Book Spotting *

Number: any number   *Age:* 8 upwards   *Time:* 3–5 minutes
Adult supervision: passing round book and setting questions
(Equipment) one book that is new to the children)

This simple game is a useful and entertaining test of the players' powers of observation. All you need do is select a book that the players are not likely to have come across before and pass it around them, telling them to take a good look at it before passing it on. No player should spend more than a minute with the book, but the passing round could take place while some other activity is going on.

When everyone has had a chance to see the book, set the players a series of questions (between 10 and 20 is fine) to see how much they remember from looking at it. You might ask them:

Who wrote the book?
What was it called?
Roughly how many pages were there?
Was there a picture on the cover?
Were there pictures inside?
Was there a price on the book, if so how much was it?
Was it a story book or one that gave information?

There will be plenty of questions you can ask about the book and they should be tailored to the age and interests of the players. The one with the highest number of correct answers wins.

Round-the-World Relay *

Number: any equal number   *Age:* 8 upwards   *Time:* 2–3 minutes   *Adult supervision:* checking answers   *(Equipment:* sheet of paper and pencil per team)

This is a geography game designed to test the players' knowledge of countries, cities, rivers, seas, mountains and other features around the world.

The players sit in two teams with the paper and pencil in front of the first player. A subject, 'Countries' perhaps, is given to the teams, and on the word 'Go!' the leader writes down a country and passes the paper and pencil to the next player, who writes down the name of a second country to the west of the first one. The third player writes down a country to the west of the second, and so on down the team until the last player has added the last country. The first team to finish wins, provided its countries do in fact lie west of each other.

The leader's choice is very important in a team's success. If *China* is chosen as the first country, the others stand a good chance of knowing countries that lie to the west of that. But a leader who writes *Chile* or *Gambia* makes it difficult for the others to follow, since many of them may not know where those countries are.

The same rules apply no matter what topics are being listed.

Just a Minute *

Number: any number   *Age:* 5 upwards   *Time:* 1 minute   *Adult supervision:* judging the minute   (*Equipment:* a watch or clock with a second hand)

All the players sit in silence. The leader holds the watch or clock and tells them when the game starts (this will be at the beginning of a complete minute). The players must then stand up when they think a minute has passed. The one who is nearest to the correct time does the timing in the next round.

Hunt the Alphabet

Number: any number   *Age:* 6 upwards   *Time:* 3–5 minutes
Adult supervision: only to explain rules and judge the 'hunt'

In this game the players work together to find objects that each represent one letter of the alphabet. They must start with something for A, an apple for instance, then something for B, perhaps the blackboard, then something for C, maybe a crayon, and so on. In some cases they may not be able to find an object for a letter. If this happens, they are allowed to improvise with what objects are available. For example, a couple of pencils used as sticks played against glasses might represent an xylophone for the letter X.

Encourage the players to use their imaginations and you will get as much fun from the game as they do.

Scrambles *

Number: any number   *Age:* 8 upwards   *Time:* 5 minutes
Adult supervision: providing scrambled words and correct answers   (*Equipment:* paper and pencil per player)

Scrambles is a game that tests the players' deductive powers as much as their memories or general knowledge. The game can involve any subject from sport to space, or from plant life to pantomimes and plays. It's also fairly simple to organize and challenging to play.

All that is required is a list of scrambled words, that is to say words with their letters arranged in the wrong order. Tell the players that the words are all connected with a specific subject, and once the list is ready allow them five minutes to write down the words in their correct spelling.

For a five minute game you will need thirty or more words, but shorter games can be played just as well with fewer words. When time is up the player with the most accurate list is allowed to choose the topic for the next game of *Scrambles*.

PLAYGROUND GAMES

King Caesar *

Number: any number   *Age:* 7 upwards   *Time:* 3–5 minutes
Adult supervision: only to prevent game from becoming
too rough

The players divide into two teams except for one player who starts the game as King Caesar (this game originated in America and that's the title they gave him there!). The two teams line up at opposite ends of the playground with King Caesar in the middle. On the word 'Go!' all the players try to dash across the open space to the other side without being caught by King Caesar. Any player who is caught is tapped on the head with the pronouncement 'I crown thee king', after which he or she joins King Caesar in trying to catch other players as they run to and fro. The last player to be caught becomes King Caesar in the next game.

American Hopscotch *

Number: 5 to a playing area   *Age:* 6 upwards   *Time:* 5–10
minutes   *Adult supervision:* explaining rules and helping to
draw playing area   (*Equipment:* some sort of marker, a piece of
tile or a shell)

Hopscotch is *Hopscotch*, or so you might think, but in spite of the widespread popularity of the British game, there is an American version which has some interesting differences, principally in the design of the

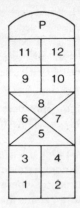

area on which it is played. This contains thirteen compartments marked out like the plan above.

Players 'pink' for the first turn, which means that they stand in the compartment marked P and throw the shell or piece of tile at the front (bottom) line of the playing area. The one whose throw lands nearest the bottom line starts. He or she stands outside the square end of the playing area and throws the shell or tile into the compartment marked 1, hops into it and kicks the shell or tile out of the playing area with the hopping foot, using any number of kicks. The player then returns to the starting position for the next turn. The other foot can be lowered now. The next throw has to land in the compartment marked 2. If the throw is success-ful, the player hops through compartment 1 into compartment 2 and again kicks out the shell or tile. The player continues like this through the compartments as far as number 8, called *rest-home*, where he or she may stand with feet astride in compartment 6 and 7 before continuing the hopping.

Until the player reaches the compartment marked P for 'plum-pudding', he or she is allowed any number of kicks to kick the shell or tile from the compartment. Once in the P compartment, however, the shell or tile has to be kicked through each of the compartments in turn back to number 1, using just one kick into each compartment and hopping through all compartments except *rest-home*. If the shell lands on a line, outside the area or in the wrong compartment, in either throwing or kicking, or if the player lets both feet touch the ground at a point where he or she should be hopping, the player is out.

The winner is the one who manages to go through the whole playing area without making a mistake.

Snail, or French Hop *

Number: 5 to a playing area   *Age:* 6 upwards   *Time:* 5–10 minutes   *Adult supervision:* explaining rules and helping to draw the playing area   (*Equipment:* some sort of marker, a piece of tile or a shell)

This is a variation of *American Hopscotch*. The same playing area is used and the rules are much the same too, but there are two major differences.

In this game players must kick the tile or shell with their hopping foot from compartment 1 into compartment 2, then into compartment 3 and so on until they reach the centre where they can put both feet on the ground (in compartments 6 and 7) once the tile or shell has been kicked into compartment 8. From here the kicking continues through all the compartments until compartment P, where the player has to turn round and kick the tile or shell back through the compartments to number 1 (again having a rest in the centre).

If a player drops a foot, kicks the tile or shell onto a line, out of the playing area, or into a wrong compartment, his turn ends and the next player has a go. But in this game too, if a player hops on a line he also forfeits his go. The winner is the player who completes the course without any mistakes.

Touch Wood and Whistle

Number: any number   *Age:* 5 upwards   *Time:* 3–5 minutes *Adult supervision:* none

This is a subtle variation of the popular game of *Touch* or *Tag*. One player is picked as It, and It has to try and catch one of the other players running round the playground. Players can avoid being caught by touching wood *and* whistling, but they must be doing both. If in the excitement of the game a player is hanging on to a piece of wood for dear life, but *not* whistling, he or she can be caught by It, which means that they must change places and the caught player sets off in pursuit of the others.

Jack, Jack, the Bread Burns

Number: any number   *Age:* 7 upwards   *Time:* 3–5 minutes
Adult supervision: only to prevent the game from becoming
too boisterous

This is for those who don't mind a little mild rough and tumble. Two of
the players are chosen to be the baker and his assistant, Jack. The rest sit
on the ground, one behind the other, and hold each other tightly round
the waist. They are the loaves in the oven.

The game begins with the baker suddenly shouting 'Jack, Jack, the
bread burns', at which he and his assistant rush to the loaves and try and
detach the first one. If they are successful that loaf is taken to the *shop*, a
previously chosen part of the playground. The other loaves can hang on
to the one being taken to prevent its removal, so the baker and Jack need
to take the loaf unawares. If the loaf manages to catch Jack or the baker
and prevent either of them from getting away, the one caught must
become a loaf and go to the back of the line.

The game continues until either all the loaves have been put in the
shop or until Jack and the baker have been caught.

The Huntsman and the Hares

Number: any number   *Age:* 6 upwards   *Time:* 3–5 minutes
Adult supervision: explaining rules

One player is chosen as the Huntsman, the others are hares. The Huntsman has to stay in prearranged bounds until the hares are ready, then he
may set off in pursuit of them. If he catches one of them, he takes the hare
back to his bounds and then they join hands and set off after more hares.
No matter how many are caught, they must always be holding hands
when they are chasing after the others.

Sevens *

Number: any number   *Age:* 7 upwards   *Time:* 3–5 minutes
Adult supervision: only to explain rules
(*Equipment:* a ball)

Sevens is a catching game in which the players must all imitate the catching action of a leader seven times. The game should begin with simple catches, the leader throwing the ball into the air and catching it with both hands seven times. The ball is then thrown to the next player, who repeats this action seven times before throwing it to the next player who does the same thing, and so the game progresses round the group.

When everyone has had a go, the leader throws the ball in a different way, catching it with one hand maybe, or turning round once before catching it. Again each of the other players must copy the leader's throwing action exactly. If anyone drops the ball during their turn they lose a point, and players who lose ten points leave the group.

The game continues, with the catches becoming progressively difficult, until only one player is left. That player becomes the leader when the game begins again.

North, South, East and West

Number: any number   *Age:* 6 upwards   *Time:* 3–5 minutes
Adult supervision: starting game as caller

Before play starts, mark out the four points of the compass in the playground. Group all the players in the centre and then call out one of the four compass points to which all the players must run. The last player there calls another compass point. The last one to this point calls another, and so on with the players dashing to and fro across the compass, and frequently swapping the role of caller as they do.

Ball Trap

Number: 6–8 per ball   *Age:* 7 upwards   *Time:* 3–5 minutes
Adult supervision: explaining game and providing balls
(*Equipment:* one ball for 6–8 players)

The players divide into their groups and one member of each is given a ball. He or she throws this into the air and calls the name of another player in the group. This player must catch the ball and shout 'Stop' if he or she is successful. (If the player misses the ball, the caller throws it again and calls another name.) All the players stop in their tracks, and the player with the ball is allowed to throw it at another player's legs. If the throw hits the legs, that player becomes the caller and starts the game again. If the ball misses, the thrower becomes the caller.

The White Spot

Number: any number   *Age:* 6 upwards   *Time:* 3–5 minutes
Adult supervision: explaining game   (*Equipment:* a piece
of chalk)

The game starts with one player being given the piece of chalk as the Lord or Lady of the White Spot. The others have to try and touch the White Spot without being marked by the chalk. At the same time, the Lord or Lady of the White Spot tries to mark the sleeves, backs or legs of the players that come within range. If the White Spot succeeds, the player marked becomes the owner of the chalk and the other joins the group of touchers.

Tag

Number: 18   *Age:* 6 upwards   *Time:* 3–5 minutes
Adult supervision: explaining game

Although there are many different versions of this time-honoured game, to play it correctly you need eighteen players who follow the rules in this way. All the players except two arrange themselves in a ring, two players deep, leaving enough space between each pair for someone to run through without difficulty.

The players out of the ring are called It and the Outplayer. The aim of the game is for It to touch the Outplayer, who can dodge in and out or round the ring, and can even take a rest by standing in front of one of the pairs inside the ring. When this happens the outside member of the ring becomes the Outplayer and has to keep out of It's way.

If the Outplayer is touched, he or she becomes It and the previous It must take the place of one of the members of a pair, as before.

Hopping Home

Number: any number   *Age:* 6 upwards   *Time:* 3–5 minutes
Adult supervision: explaining game

Two 'homes' are marked out at either end of the playground and a small area is marked between them as the 'castle'. All the players but one stand in one of the homes, the odd one out is the King or Queen who must stand in the castle. On the word 'Go!' the players in the home have to hop across the playground to the opposite home, while the King or Queen hops around the playground trying to catch them.

Any player who is caught becomes a soldier and has to help catch the other players. Players who let both feet touch the ground as they hop from one home to the other become soldiers too. But if the King, or Queen, lets both feet touch the ground while trying to catch the others, he or she must go back to the castle before setting out again to touch the players.

The game ends when all the players have become soldiers.

PLAYING-FIELD GAMES

Feeder

Number: any number   *Age:* 7 upwards   *Time:* 10 minutes or
longer   *Adult supervision:* helping to mark out ground
(*Equipment:* soft ball, markers for bases)

This American game amounts to a simplified form of baseball. One of the
players is chosen to be Feeder, and he or she occupies the Feeder Station
in the middle of the playing area. Around the outside of the circular
pitch are five equally spaced markers or bases, and the one in front of the
Feeder Station is the Home base.

At the start of the game, the Feeder is given the ball and the other
players line up at the Home base. The Feeder throws the ball underarm to
the first of the players who must hit it with the open palm of the hand as
far as possible, in order to be able to run to the first base, and ideally
round all of the bases. The Feeder should try to pick up the ball and
throw it at the player while he or she is running. If the ball hits the player,
then he or she is out and has to leave the game.

If the first player stops at the first base, he or she must run on when
the second player has hit the ball, because two players may not stand on
the same base (except for the Home base).

If the Feeder catches a ball hit by one of the players, that player
becomes the Feeder, and the previous Feeder has a chance to hit the ball
with the rest. The same happens if any player fails to hit the ball thrown
by the Feeder.

Whoop

Number: any number   *Age:* 6 upwards   *Time:* 5–10 minutes
Adult supervision: none (unless acting as the Seeker)

One of the players is chosen as the Seeker who waits at a place known as
Home with eyes closed until all the other players have hidden in various
places. The last to hide cries 'Whoop' to tell the Seeker to open his or her
eyes and start hunting for the others. The hiders must try to steal back to
Home without being caught. If they manage to do this, they may hide
again. The first to be caught becomes the Seeker in the next round.

Balloon Tennis *

Number: 2 or 4 *Age:* 5 upwards *Time:* 5–10 minutes
Adult supervision: umpiring (*Equipment:* two poles, a length
of string, several inflated balloons)

This is an enjoyable playing-field game for small groups of players. The
poles and string represent the tennis net and can be rigged up in a couple
of minutes. The players take their sides, either in singles or doubles play.
The umpire throws the balloon to one side who hit it over the 'net' with
their hands, trying to make it land on the ground on the other side. The
receiving players hit the balloon back over the 'net' in such a way that it
will land on the ground on that side.

Every time the balloon touches the ground, the team who hit it score
one point and the first team to score five points wins.

Crab Scuttle Relay *

Number: any even number *Age:* 6 upwards *Time:* 2–3
minutes *Adult supervision:* umpiring

Before this game begins, a course is set up along which the players must
race. Two equal teams are formed and line up one behind the other on
the starting line. On the word 'Go!' the first player in each team runs to
the end of the course and back again. He then bends over and with his left
hand through his legs, grabs the hand of the player behind. They run
down the course like this, looking like crabs. When these two return to
the team, the second player bends down, and with his hand through his
legs takes the hand of the third player. Again they scuttle down the
course and back again. In the end the whole team has to scuttle down to
one end and back to the starting line once more.

The first team to complete the course like this wins.

Whack and Catch

Number: any number *Age:* 8 upwards *Time:* 5–10 minutes
Adult supervision: none (*Equipment:* a rounders or baseball bat
and a tennis ball)

In this game the players take it in turns to have an 'innings', standing at one point in the field with the bat in one hand and the ball in the other. The batsman has three 'goes' at throwing the ball in the air and hitting it with the bat. If he or she misses after the third go, the bat must be dropped and the other players can rush forward to pick it up. Whoever manages to get there first has a turn at batting.

The rest of the players are spread round the field in the hope of catching the ball after it has been hit. Again anyone who does this takes a turn with the bat. If the ball sails past the fielders without being caught, they chase after it and throw it from where they stop it to the place where the batsman is standing. He or she must drop the bat after hitting the ball and stand clear as the fielder then has to try and hit the bat with the ball. If the throw is successful the fielder has a go at batting, but if it misses, the batsman carries on as before.

Kangaroo Racing *

Number: any number   *Age:* 6 upwards   *Time:* 2–3 minutes
Adult supervision: judging race   (*Equipment:* one inflated
balloon per player)

The players line up on the starting line each with a balloon between the knees, and on the word 'Go!' they must start hopping down the course like kangaroos, being careful not to drop the balloons as they go. Any player who drops a balloon must catch it, put it back between the knees and start racing again from the point where the balloon fell.

The first player across the line with the balloon intact wins.

Handkerchief *

Number: any even number   *Age:* 6 upwards   *Time:* 2–3
minutes   *Adult supervision:* judging results   (*Equipment:* one
handkerchief per player)

This is a game of speed and agility that has been a favourite with Boy Scout troops for generations. At the start of the game all the players tuck a handkerchief through the back of their belts or inside the waistband of their trousers. The handkerchiefs are not tied in any way, so they can be pulled out easily by crafty opponents.

The players are divided into two teams and line up facing one another. They then pair off and move into an open space to start the contest. At the word 'Go!' each player has to try and grab his opponent's handkerchief while protecting his own one at the same time. The rules prevent players from backing up against trees or buildings or from lying on the ground.

The team with the most handkerchiefs at the end of the game is the winner.

Pall Mall *

Number: any number   *Age:* 8 upwards   *Time:* 5–10 minutes
Adult supervision: providing equipment and positioning
hoops   (*Equipment:* 2 iron hoops, a ball and mallet (any
suitable bat or stick will do))

Pall Mall was originally known as Paille Maille in the seventeenth century, when it was very popular. It is seldom played today, which is a pity because it is far simpler than croquet which grew out of it.

A fairly smooth stretch of grass is needed for the game, and the two iron hoops are stuck in the ground at either end of this. The first player is given the ball and mallet, and the aim is to drive the ball through the two hoops in the fewest number of strokes. The player who does this scores one point. The game is played for an agreed number of rounds, at the end of which the player with the highest score is the winner.

Rounders *

Number: 20 *Age:* 8 upwards   *Time:* 15–30 minutes   *Adult*
supervision: acting as umpire   (*Equipment:* markers for five
bases, bat and tennis ball)

The correct number with which to play *Rounders* is twenty, ten on each side. The leaders of both sides toss a coin to see which one will start 'in' and which 'out'. The field contains five bases marked out as a pentagon with base number 1 (Home base) at the top. The Feeder throws the ball from the Feeder line which is also marked on the pitch.

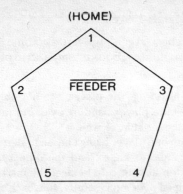

(HOME)

The batting side (the 'ins') line up one behind the other at the Home base while the 'outs', except for the Feeder, spread out around the field. Each batsman is allowed three chances to hit the ball. If he or she misses three times the umpire calls 'out' and the player leaves the batting side for that innings. When the ball is hit, the striker must drop the bat immediately for the next player and must run round the bases back to the Home base. If any member of the fielding side manages to hit the player with the ball while he or she is running, or hits a base before the player reaches it, the player is also given out; so are players who hit catches.

A player who is able to run all the way round the pitch back to Home base scores one run for his or her side, and joins the back of the line to bat again. The side with highest score is the winner.

Hop, Step and Jump *

Number: any number   *Age:* 7 upwards   *Time:* 3–5 minutes
Adult supervision: umpiring

The aim of this athletic field game is to be the one who covers the greatest distance with a hop, a step and a jump. Players may approach the take-off line at a run if they wish, but they must all start their hop from the same point, and the step and jump must follow immediately afterwards. The one who goes furthest is the winner.

Clear the Mark Leap-Frog *

Number: any number   *Age:* 7 upwards   *Time:* 5–10 minutes
Adult supervision: none   (*Equipment:* a strip of material to
act as a marker)

In this version of leap-frog, the players are not only concerned with
clearing the back of the player bending over, but they have to try and
clear a marker on the far side as well.

Play begins with one player being chosen to start as the 'back'. He or
she bends over, hands on knees, and the others take it in turns to
leap-frog over the top, taking care to clear the marker on the far side.
When all have jumped over successfully, the 'back' moves back a pace
from the marker and the others all jump over again. The game continues
like this until one player fails to clear the marker. He then becomes the
'back'. If another player fails to clear the mark in the same round he has to
take over as the 'back'. The player who is the 'back' at the end of a round
moves back a pace to start the next round. Only players who have cleared
the mark successfully now try to clear it at the new distance. The game
follows this pattern until none of the players are able to leap-frog over
the 'back' and clear the mark, which will have got some way from the
'back' by now.

Square Chasing

Number: any even number   *Age:* 6 upwards   *Time:* 3–5
minutes   *Adult supervision:* calling instructions

The players divide into four teams and each forms one side of a square.
The caller goes along each team numbering the players, so that there are
four players (one from each team) with the same number.

Play starts with the caller calling a number. The four players whose
number it is set off round the outside of the square in a clockwise
direction trying to catch each other. The caller can reverse their direction by shouting 'Change!', and when a player is caught they all return to
their places and another number is called to start the game again.

Jolly Miller

Number: any number   *Age:* 6 upwards   *Time:* 2–3 minutes
Adult supervision: acting as caller

All the players but one form a double circle with the players standing in
pairs. The odd one out stands in the middle as the Jolly Miller. Play
begins with the caller telling the circle to start walking round. They do
this until the leader calls 'Grab!', whereupon the inner circle must move
up one place allowing the Jolly Miller a chance to slip into the inner
circle and gain a place. If he or she does this, the player pushed out of the
inner circle becomes the Jolly Miller.

PARTY GAMES

Planning a Children's Party
Parlour Games
Musical Games
Racing Games
Talking Games
Acting Games
Paper and Pencil Games
Home Entertainment

PLANNING A CHILDREN'S PARTY

Planning a successful children's party calls for the skill of a conjuror, the tact of a diplomat, the stamina of a decathlete and the self-control of an umpire. Children, unlike most adults, expect entertainment at their parties; it's the reason they go to them. Parties that aren't fun are worse than no parties at all.

That said, a well-planned children's party, approached with enthusiasm and forethought can be a most rewarding family occasion. If the children are under three years old, it also gives you the chance to make friends with like-minded parents with children of the same age as yours.

While no two parties are exactly the same, there are certain well-tried guidelines that have saved sleepless nights and eleventh-hour panics. Here is a checklist of the essentials to be borne in mind at the outset of your plans, remembering that they vary according to the age-group and that they are concerned with indoor parties and may not necessarily be applicable to picnics and barbecues.

1. Use the opportunity to invite every child whose parties have been attended by your children.
2. You may feel you should invite certain relatives, even if they decide not to come.
3. Make sure there are prizes for competitive games and paper and pencils for writing games, making sure there are enough to go round. Wrap up a 'parcel' if Pass The Parcel is to be played.
4. It is a nice gesture to send every child home with a small present. This ends the party with a climax and marks a definite cut-off point.
5. Take sensible precautions in those rooms where the party will be held. It isn't fair on the children or yourself to leave valuable ornaments or fragile furnishings in rooms where party games will be played.
6. No birthday party is complete without a cake and the right number of candles. Remember the matches but keep them out of reach. It is also a good idea to buy everlasting candles that relight themselves when blown out. To small children these seem like magic.
7. Photographs of the occasion are almost as essential as the cake, but often something you only remember when the table is laid

and everyone is sitting down! Equip your camera with film and flashes before the party starts.

8. If parents are staying with very young children, don't forget they'll want something to eat and drink too. With older children, decide in advance whether they are to be met 'at the door' or parents are to be invited in for a drink, and if so let them know by phone or on the invitation.

Planning Tips

This a checklist of requirements that you can tailor to your own needs. You may not need them at every party, but you'll probably need them all at some time in your children's party years.

1. Make a list of children (including your own) to enable you to estimate the amount of food, presents, balloons, etc

2. Attractive invitations, addressed to each child, add to the sense of occasion. Avoid giving your child invitations to hand out at school unless you intend inviting the whole class!

3. Balloons for use as decorations and gifts.

4. Crackers (if bought after Christmas they may be cheaper) and streamers are colourful and fun.

5. Party hats if the crackers don t contain them.

6. Whistles and blowers only if you can put up with the noise.

7. Small cheap prizes, eg funny paper masks, coloured pencils. Don't get into competition with other parents over these.

8. Small gifts to give out at the end: one per child and preferably all alike. Small bags of sweets and colouring books are fine. It is a good idea to let your child, as host, hand them out.

9. Music with a good beat, ideally a portable cassette player that you can control for games such as musical bumps and musical chairs.

10. Candles, candle-holders and matches for the cake (if a birthday).

11. Plenty of kitchen paper and tissues for very young children.

12. Paper plates, mugs (or cans of drink and straws saves spillages, napkins, and table-cloths (you can get attractive matching sets).

13. Dustbin liners for collecting rubbish.

14. Lay the table, and make sure there are enough chairs, well in advance.

15. Make a list of games in the order in which they are to be played.

Balance noisy and quiet games and keep a 'sitting down game' for after tea.

Food and Drink

Here lies the major difference between adult and children's parties, and for once this is easier; managed properly it can be the easiest catering of all. If your party is going well, most guests will be too excited to eat very much, and if you are planning further strenuous or active games after tea they shouldn't eat too much anyway.

At the centre of the spread comes the cake, usually an object of visual rather than gastronomic admiration. In other words don't spend a fortune on exotic ingredients they probably won't like anyway, your guests will enjoy a simple cake just as well. What counts is the decoration and here you should try and be original. Chocolate or lemon frosting is usually popular. Most children don't like marzipan. A model of a space rocket (or whatever the current craze is), carefully sculpted from a supermarket sponge-cake will be just as great a success as one that takes far longer to prepare and costs more into the bargain.

One of the easiest ideas for a birthday cake for young children is to design one in the shape of the child's age, ie 5 or 6. This can be simply and cheaply done with mini-chocolate rolls (make sure you use enough for everyone to have one to eat). Finally, don't forget to leave room for the candleholders.

Savouries will probably prove more popular than sandwiches with your young guests, which is a blessing for you since they can be prepared easily and quickly. Keep these simple too. Sausages on sticks (at least three per child), pizza (bought fresh that day, cut into small slices and heated) will satisfy most children. Similarly masses of crisps, pineapple and cheese on cocktail sticks, small cakes, chocolate biscuits and ice-creams (served right at the end of the party just before they all leave), require little effort on your part and will keep your guests happy. Decide on your drinks (cans or jugs of squash) and have plenty.

The Party Itself – What To Do

Since the rest of this chapter is filled with games for all ages, it is only necessary to give an outline here of the type of entertainment you might give to different age groups.

Naturally you will want to celebrate each of your child's birthdays, but in the early years (1 and 2 at least) this need not involve anyone outside the immediate family and those who have helped through the difficult first twelve months. Invite them for tea or a drink and cut a small cake with one candle on it. If the birthday falls at a week-end, you might consider a small lunch party to celebrate the occasion.

Your child may well have made friends at a playgroup by the age of three and these should obviously be invited to the third birthday party. So should other children (cousins perhaps) who are less frequent visitors. Depending on your own child and the confidence of the others, you may try some very simple games. However, at this age most children are happier still left to their own devices.

It's at four that your duties as master or mistress of ceremonies begin in earnest, and from that age until eight or nine you can reckon on filling your parties with games featured in the pages that follow, increasing in sophistication as you advance up the age-scale. The more originality you can introduce, the more fun your parties will be. Fancy dress, 'themes' based on popular television programmes or the latest *Superman* film, hired entertainers or home video cartoons will all add colour to your parties. Behind the most lavish amusements there must still be a well-planned structure. In the final analysis satisfaction and not sophistication must be your goal, and if your guests go home tired and happy after playing nothing but Blind Man's Buff and Sardines all afternoon, you have no cause to think your party anything but a total success. You can even celebrate by going out yourselves in the evening to recharge your batteries; so add finding a baby-sitter to the bottom of your checklist!

PARLOUR GAMES

Fish Pond

Number: any even number   *Age:* any age (ideal for 8–9)   *Time:* as long as it takes to pair children   *Adult supervision:* only to keep game moving   (*Equipment:* pencil tied to long piece of string for each boy)

This is an ideal pairing game to match boys and girls for subsequent games involving couples. The girls all go out of the room, leaving the door open only a few inches. One after another the boys 'cast' their fishing lines, by throwing their pencils tied to a length of string over the top of the door. The girls take it in turns to catch the pencils and are reeled in by their new partners. When all have been paired, the next game can begin at once.

Initial I-Spy

Number: any number *Age:* any age *Time:* as long as it takes to introduce all the guests to each other *Adult supervision:* none necessary, except to give encouragement to the timid

This game gets over the formal business of introducing children to each other, and gives them a chance to find out what each other's names are while having fun at the same time. It's a game too in which the host child can begin play to encourage the guests to join in. Each child starts by telling the others his or her first name. Then, in no more than a minute, he or she must name as many objects in the room that begin with the initial of that name. So if David stands up he might see a door, a dog, a dish, a diary and a dinner-plate. When all the guests have had a go, they should have some idea of what the others are called.

The Floating Feather *(optional)

Number: any number *Age:* 5–8 *Time:* as many rounds as the children want *Adult supervision:* supplying feathers and judging when the feather lands on the floor *(Equipment:* several light feathers (swansdown))

Although one feather is really all that this game requires, it's as well to have a few more in reserve in case your first one goes missing after Round One.

The players start by standing in a small circle and the feather is dropped from above into the centre. They have to keep it in the air for as long as they can by moving underneath it and blowing at it as hard as they can. When the feather eventually lands a new round begins. Adults can keep a counting or timed record of each round to see how long the group can keep the feather aloft.

The game can be played with as much fun by older children using a balloon. The rules are exactly the same, though if you want to make the game competitive every child must have their own balloon. The last one to let a balloon touch the floor is the winner.

Cat and Mouse

Number: any equal number   *Age:* 7–10   *Time:* at least four
rounds   *Adult supervision:* needed to call the 'changes'
(*Equipment:* possibly a whistle or gong)

Here is a version of this popular game from Central Africa. The players
form three or four parallel lines of equal numbers, after two have been
chosen as cat and mouse. The players in the lines form arches by raising
their arms and holding hands with the players standing next to them. At
the given signal (by voice, whistle or gong), the mouse starts dodging
between the arches and down the rows with the cat in hot pursuit. On the
order to 'change', the players in the lines turn to their left through a
quarter of a circle and form new arches with the players now standing
next to them. The lines need to change position very quickly when the
command is given. This is meant to confuse the cat in its pursuit of the
mouse. The game continues in this way until the mouse is caught. Then
two more players become cat and mouse and the game continues for
another round.

Squeak, Piggy, Squeak

Number: 6 or more   *Age:* 5 and upwards   *Time:* 10 minutes or
more   *Adult supervision:* turning round blindfolded player and
making sure he or she doesn't fall during the game
(*Equipment:* a blindfold)

If you want a quick, simple, hilarious game to get everyone rolling about
with laughter, or to revive a flagging party, you can't do much better than
play this one. It works well with six players but is even more fun if there
are more to join in.

One player is blindfolded and stands in the middle of the room. The
others sit round in a circle, cross-legged. Spin the blindfolded player
three times. He or she must then walk to the edge of the circle and when
one of the seated players is reached, the blindfolded player must sit in
that player's lap and say 'Squeak, Piggy, squeak!'

The player now squeaks, disguising his or her voice as much as
possible to prevent the blindfolded player from guessing who it is. If the
guess is correct the players change places. If not, the blindfolded player
is lead back to the centre of the circle to have another go.

Pennies in the Circle *

Number: any even number   *Age:* 7–11   *Time:* 5–10 minutes
Adult supervision: to judge accuracy of players
(Equipment: a lot of pennies (4 per player) and a piece of chalk)

As a cross between Shove Halfpenny and curling, this is a useful game to keep up your sleeve for parties that might have taken place in the garden – if it wasn't raining. Provided you have a hard floor surface where chalk marks don't matter, you can amuse children with this knock-out game of skill and accuracy.

Draw a chalk circle about 15 cms (6 inches) in diameter at one end of the playing area, and line the players up, two by two, at the opposite end. Players must kneel down and try to slide each of their four pennies into the chalk circle. Only one player from each pair goes into the next round: the one who gets the most pennies in the circle or, failing any bullseyes, the one who lands pennies nearest the circle. The losing partner from each pair drops out after each turn.

In the next round the winning players again pair off and play again, and the game continues with the elimination of one player after each turn until only two players are left to play in the final, which is won by the better shot. A small prize is awarded, a chocolate coin maybe?

Farmyard

Number: 4 or more   *Age:* 4–6   *Time:* as long as your imagination can keep the story going   *Adult supervision:* allocating names and telling story

If you can possibly persuade young children to play a quiet game immediately after tea, there is far less likelihood of any upsets. *Farmyard* should fit the bill nicely, providing you're up to it after serving the tea!

The players sit on the floor, and you give each one the name of a farmyard animal or bird that has a noise that a child can imitate without difficulty. If you run out of names, repeat some of the ones you've already used; most farms have more than one of each animal after all.

Now comes the tricky bit. You have to tell a farmyard story bringing in all the animals you've just named. Each time you mention an animal, that player (or players) must make the animal's sound. Periodically include the phrase 'And they all woke up' at which all the animals make their noises at once.

Hop Rabbit Hop! *

Number: any number   *Age:* younger children up to 5   *Time:* 5–10 minutes   *Adult supervision:* stopping and starting the game and judging who is out

All the players become rabbits in this game. If you like, you can start by asking each its name. These must be real rabbit names, Peter, Benjamin, Thumper, Bugs, Hazel etc. – non-rabbit names aren't allowed. With very young children, though, it's probably easier to dispense with the names. Ask the players to get into rabbit positions, squatting down with their arms clasped round their knees. When the game begins they have to hop about in this position until you shout 'Stop!' (If you prefer, you can use a cassette recorder with a tape of *Run, Rabbit, Run,* or other appropriate music.) Whatever signal you give, the rabbits must freeze for ten seconds without moving until you say 'Hop rabbit hop', and start your music again.

   Any rabbit who carries on hopping, falls over or moves in any other way during the 'freeze' period, leaves the game. The last rabbit left hopping is the winner. Give him a lettuce leaf as a prize!

Blind Man's Buff

Number: any number   *Age:* any age   *Time:* as many rounds as the players want   *Adult supervision:* enough to prevent Blind Man from causing damage to himself, herself, or the room (*Equipment:* a blindfold)

Blind Man's Buff is almost as old as play itself. The game has been enjoyed by players all over the world for thousands of years. There are many variations but the traditional British method goes like this.

   One of the players (the host child perhaps) is chosen as the Blind Man and is blindfolded and stands in the middle of the room. The other children then chant: 'How many horses has your father got?'

   'Three!' answers the Blind Man.
   'What colours are they?' ask the others.
   'Black, white and grey!' replies the Blind Man.
   'Turn round three times and catch who you may!' say the others.

The Blind Man turns round three times and then tries to catch one of the players who are, of course, trying to keep out the way. When one is caught, that player changes places with the Blind Man and the next round begins as before.

The traditional verse is best left out for young players unless they can remember it, but it does add fun to the game if the players can manage it.

Safety is an important consideration too. Make sure that precious objects (if not already removed) are put well out of harm's way before the Blind Man sets off in pursuit of his victims. Check too that tables with sharp edges and anything that might cause a child to trip and fall are removed from the centre of action. If there isn't already a guard in front of an open fire, put one there.

Blind Man's Buff is a simple, fast, energetic way of getting a party going, though keep an eye out for any tomboys who throw their weight about. Their energies can be tactfully diverted before the party really gets into top gear.

Hunt the Thimble

Number: any number   *Age:* 6 and above   *Time:* 5 minutes
Adult supervision: hiding thimble and keeping time
(*Equipment:* a thimble)

Still as popular as it was when it was first played hundreds of years ago, *Hunt the Thimble* sounds a much easier game to play than it turns out to be in reality. All the players leave the room, the door is closed and the key-hole blocked. The thimble is then placed anywhere in the room, providing that it isn't out of sight. The players come in again and start searching for the thimble. Those who find it say nothing but sit down very quietly. After five minutes of searching, the game ends and anyone left standing can pay a forfeit (standing on one leg for a minute, for example).

Grandmother's Footsteps

Number: any number   *Age:* 5–8   *Time:* as many rounds as the
players want   *Adult supervision:* judging who moves in the
case of any dispute

Like many of the world's most popular games this is simple and very
exciting to play. Although called *Grandmother's Footsteps* in Britain,
the same game is known as *Grandpa's Footsteps* or *Who's Afraid of the
Big Bad Wolf?* in North America, so if there are any objections to playing
Grandmother, just give the game another name!

One of the players is selected as Grandmother and stands at one end
of the room facing the wall. The other players line up at the other end and
on the word 'Go' start creeping slowly and silently towards Granny. If
Granny thinks she hears anyone moving, she turns round suddenly. All
the players must freeze until Granny turns back to the wall before
continuing their stealthy progress. Anyone caught moving has to go
back to the starting line and begin again. The game continues in this way
with players creeping forward when Granny's back is turned and freezing when she whips round, until one of them gets close enough to touch
her on the shoulder. That player becomes the next Granny.

Blind Man's Treasure Hunt

Number: any number   *Age:* 3–7   *Time:* 5–10 minutes   *Adult
supervision:* blindfolding players and leading them to parcels
(Equipment: as many parcels as players)

The more effort you put into preparing this game, the more fun it is, so be
ready to spend some time wrapping the parcels the night before the
party. Start by sending all the players out of the room. While they are
outside lay out the parcels on the floor in the middle of the room. Lead in
the players one by one, having blindfolded them outside the door. Each
player may choose one parcel which can only be unwrapped when all
the players have chosen theirs. When everyone is back in the room and
sitting on the floor with their parcels, tell them to remove their blindfolds and start unwrapping. Here your preparation adds to the fun. Some
of the parcels will be large, some will be small, but all should be
thoroughly wrapped with plenty of paper and sticky tape. Put something rather nice – a sweet, a toy brooch or ring in the smaller parcels,
and pack surprises like large stones, a potato or an old shoe in the large

ones. Greedy players get a rude shock when they discover what they have chosen!

(It's as well to have a large cardboard box or a dustbin liner ready to collect the waste-paper after this game.)

The Donkey's Tail *

Number: any number *Age:* 5–8 *Time:* 5 minutes *Adult supervision:* preparation of donkey and tail (*Equipment:* drawing of a donkey, donkey's tail and some means of attachment)

You may think the amount of effort involved in preparation isn't merited by the game itself, but you have only to see the enjoyment that children get from playing it to convince yourself that a quarter of an hour (or slightly more depending on your draughtsmanship) is a small price to pay. There's also no reason why the picture and tail can't be used at future parties.

The object of the game is delightfully simple. Each of the players is blindfolded in turn, given the donkey's tail and told to stick this in the right place on the picture of the donkey. This is pretty difficult when they can't see what they are doing.

It's up to you how elaborate you make your donkey and tail. You can draw a donkey (minus tail) on a large sheet of paper and stick this to a piece of hardboard hung on the back of a door. The tail can be made from a piece of strong card or string or plaited wool with a blob of adhesive putty to avoid making holes in your paintwork. On the other hand a rough sketch of a donkey drawn on a children's blackboard with a piece of paper for a tail serves just as well.

Blindfold the first player. Give him the tail and lead him towards the donkey. Leave the player to stick the tail on the donkey and then let the player take off the blindfold and see where the tail has landed. The poor donkey is likely to have tails growing in some fairly odd places – but this is the fun of the game. Keep a note of who sticks the tail closest to the correct position and when everyone has had a go, give a small prize (a chocolate donkey, perhaps) to the winner.

Winking

Number: 10 or more   *Age:* 9 upwards   *Time:* at least two
rounds, one with girls sitting, one with boys   *Adult
supervision:* necessary only to see that the rules are followed
(*Equipment:* half as many chairs as players plus an extra chair)

This game can be used to get a party started as well as to play during the
main run of games. Make a circle of chairs facing inwards. Seat a girl on
every chair except one. Boys stand behind all the chairs, including the
vacant one. Their hands rest on the back of the chairs but must not touch
the girl sitting in front of them.

The boy standing behind the vacant chair starts the game by winking at one of the girls. She must immediately try to dash from her chair to
his. The boy standing behind her must try to stop her before she makes
off by placing his hands on her shoulders. If he succeeds, the girl must
remain seated and the boy behind the vacant chair has to try winking at
another girl. However, if the girl does manage to get away, the boy who
failed to stop her must now try winking at one of the other girls. A few
goes will soon show that it is the quick, subtle wink that wins the girl!

Once the girls have been winked at, let the boys sit down and repeat
the game with the girls winking at them.

Spinning the Plate *

Number: 4 or more   *Age:* 5 and upwards   *Time:* 5 to 10
minutes   *Adult supervision:* allocation of names and checking
each moves at the right moment   (*Equipment:* an unbreakable
plate)

The players sit in a circle and each is given the name of a bird, a flower,
an animal, or, if your party has a special theme, a name connected with
that theme. If young children are playing, it may be better not to give
them names at all. They can play just as well using their own first names.
Older children enjoy having different names and it keeps them on their
toes.

Place the plate in the middle of the circle. Step out of the circle and
call out one of the names. That player then has to rush to the plate, pick it
up and start it spinning. The moment it is spinning he calls out another
name and hurries back to his seat. The player whose name has just been
called has to catch the plate before it stops spinning and then spins it

again, calling another player's name at the same time. Play continues in this way, with every player having a chance at spinning the plate.

Any player who fails to catch the plate in time drops out. The last player left spinning the plate is the winner.

MUSICAL GAMES

Musical Arches *

Number: any even number   *Age:* 4–9   *Time:* 5 minutes   *Adult supervision:* controlling music   (*Equipment:* source of music (ideally a portable cassette recorder))

Two pairs of players, one standing at each end of the room, join hands and raise them above their heads to form an arch. All the other players line up in pairs and dance through the two arches while the music plays. As soon as the music stops the arches lower their arms to catch any pairs passing through. Any pair caught by an arch has to form another arch itself. The game continues in this way until every pair but one has been caught. The remaining pair are the winners.

The game can be played for as many rounds as the players wish.

Paul Jones

Number: any number   *Age:* any age   *Time:* enough rounds to get everyone introduced   *Adult supervision:* controlling music   (*Equipment:* source of music)

This game is a variation of the ice-breaking dance which has been a traditional way of introducing guests who may not know each other. It can be played at the start of a party to get everyone in the mood, and only requires a little light-hearted imagination on the part of the controlling adult to make it an hilarious opening to a good party.

The players form two circles, one inside the other, with the boys on the outside facing inwards and the girls on the inside facing outwards. When the music plays, the two circles dance round in opposite directions. As soon as it stops, the boys and girls facing each other form pairs and must perform whatever task is set for them by the controlling adult. Don't make these tasks too complicated or embarrassing; a handshake, spinning each other round a few times, standing on one leg and hopping in a circle, anything quick and lively will do as long as it keeps the game moving. Start the music as soon as the pairs have finished, with the circles forming once more and moving in opposite directions. Let the game continue like this until most players have been introduced.

Musical Hotch-Potch *

Number: 4 or more   *Age:* 4–8   *Time:* 3–5 minutes   *Adult supervision:* controlling music, removing articles and judging players   (*Equipment:* source of music and a selection of small everyday items: small toys, sweets, nuts, fruit)

Place the articles selected for the game in the centre of the playing area, making sure that there is one fewer than the number of players. Start the music and tell the players to hop round the pile in time to the music; get them to hop clockwise to avoid confusion. When the music stops they must dive for the pile and grab one item each. The player who fails to grab an item leaves the circle and you remove one of the articles before starting the music for the second round. The contest continues until only two players are left in the game with one object remaining. The one who takes this as the music stops is the winner, and can keep it as a prize.

Musical Bumps *

Number: 4 or more   *Age:* 4 upwards   *Time:* 2–5 minutes *Adult supervision:* controlling music and judging players (*Equipment:* source of music)

The players form a circle and jump up and down while the music plays. As soon as it stops they must fall to the ground and sit cross-legged. The last player in this position must drop out. The game continues until only the one player is left who becomes the winner.

Oranges and Lemons

Number: 8 or more (the more the merrier)   *Age:* 6 upwards
Time: 5 minutes or longer   *Adult supervision:* leading
singing and possibly forming the arch

Either two grown-ups or two of the tallest children form an arch by
joining hands and holding their arms up high. Before the game starts
they decide who will be the orange and who the lemon. The other
players form a chain, each holding on to the waist of the player in front.
They pass through the arch singing the traditional song *Oranges and
Lemons.* (With younger children the adults will need to lead the singing
and probably call the lines as they come up – the children will manage
the tune for themselves!) On the final word of the song, 'head', the pair
forming the arch drop their arms and catch the child passing underneath. The child is asked in a whisper which of the two sides of the arch
he or she wishes to join – Oranges or Lemons. Having decided, the child
holds on to that player's waist and the song beins again.

Ideally an equal number of Oranges and Lemons will be built up as
the game progresses, so that when the last player has been caught, the
two sides can have a tug of war!

Here are the words of the song, which you might like to copy out to
give to other adults watching the game. They might as well join in with
the singing to make it more fun for all:

> Oranges and lemons
> Say the bells of St Clement's.
> Bulls'-eyes and targets
> Say the bells of St Margaret's.
> Brickbats and tiles
> Say the bells of St Giles.
> Pancakes and fritters
> Say the bells of St Peter's.
> Two sticks and an apple
> Say the bells of Whitechapel.
> Old Father Baldpate
> Say the slow bells of Aldgate.
> Maids in white aprons
> Say the bells of St Catherine's.
> Pokers and tongs
> Say the bells of St John's.
> Kettles and pans
> Say the bells of St Anne's.

You owe me five farthings
Say the bells of St Martin's.
When will you pay me?
Say the bells of Old Bailey.
When I grow rich
Say the bells of Shoreditch.
Pray, when will that be?
Say the bells of Stepney.
I'm sure I don't know
Says the great bell of Bow. } *(Sing these lines slowly.)*
Here comes a candle to light you to bed
Here comes a chopper to chop off your head!

Musical Islands *

Number: any number   *Age:* 5 upwards   *Time:* 5 minutes
Adult supervision: controlling the music and judging players
(Equipment: source of music and sheets of newspaper, one
fewer than the number of players)

Scatter the sheets of newspaper (islands) around the playing area. Start
the music and get the players to dance around the floor, covering as much
ground as they can but not stepping on the 'islands'. Stop the music and
see which player is the last to leap onto an 'island' for safety. Whoever
fails to get his or her feet on 'dry land' has to drop out. Remove one of the
islands and start the music again. The game continues like this until all
but one of the players has been eliminated. That one is the winner.

Musical Reflexes *

Number: any number   *Age:* 7 upwards   *Time:* 3–5 minutes
depending on number of players   *Adult supervision:* judging
players and scoring   *(Equipment:* source of music (ideally a
portable cassette player))

Invite one of the players to operate the music (maybe the host should
start by doing this). The music operator stands with his back facing the
other players, but in full view of them. All the players face the operator's
back and sit on the floor. The operator switches on the music, and the

other players have to guess when the operator is going to switch off the music. They stand up at the moment when they think the music is about to be turned off. Of course, it is very hard to guess the exact moment and some players will stand up far too soon, while others will still be sitting when the music suddenly cuts off. The music operator has to disguise the switching off by using exaggerated or false movements to confuse the other players.

The last one to rise before the music ends is the winner of that round and gets one point. Any players left sitting when the music ends lose a point. The first player to reach a total of five points is the winner and can operate the music in the next game.

Musical Chairs *

Number: 6 or more   *Age:* any age   *Time:* 5 minutes
Adult supervision: controlling music and removing chairs
(*Equipment:* chairs, one fewer than the number of players,
source of music)

Place the chairs in a circle with the seats facing outwards. The players hold hands and form a ring round the chairs. When the music starts they must dance round in a circle, but the moment the music stops, the players must drop into the nearest chair. The player who is slowest will find there are no seats left and must drop out of the game, taking away one of the chairs. The game continues like this with one player and one seat leaving every time the music stops. The player who is left sitting on the last chair is the winner.

Musical Walking Stick *

Number: 4 or more   *Age:* 5–8   *Time:* under 5 minutes
Adult supervision: controlling music and judging players
(*Equipment:* source of music and a walking stick)

Choose a stick which suits the size of the players. If you don't have a walking stick to hand, an umbrella or a garden cane will do.

Sit all the players in a circle on the floor and give the stick to one of them. Start the music and tell the player with the stick to tap one end on the floor three times and then pass it to the player on the right. This player must also tap the stick three times before passing it on in a clockwise direction, with each player tapping the stick three times before parting with it. The player caught holding the stick when the music stops leaves the circle.

The knock-out process continues until only one player is left in the game. That player is the winner.

Musical Statues *

Number: 4 or more *Age:* 4–11 *Time:* 3–5 minutes
Adult supervision: controlling music and judging movements
(*Equipment:* source of music)

The last thing most children want to do at a party is stand stock still, which makes this party game one of the most teasing and most popular. It works particularly well if you contrast the 'freezing' with lively energetic music.

Start the music and get all the children to dance around the room. At first play the music for quite a long time to get them in the mood. When the music does stop, so must the children. They must freeze in their tracks. Not a foot, not a hand, not a head must move. They mustn't giggle wobble, twitch or bat an eyelid. Anyone who does move has to leave the game. Keep a sharp look-out while the music has stopped, but don't prolong the agony with younger children, and keep the freezing period short in the early stages anyway. Start the music again and encourage them to dance about. Then stop it again and repeat the formula. Gradually lengthen the freezing period to make the game more difficult as the players drop out. The one left at the end is the winner. (Why not let that player work the music in the next game?)

The Grand Old Duke of York

Number: 8 or more *Age:* 5–8 *Time:* 3–5 minutes *Adult supervision:* possibly leading in the singing (*Equipment:* source of music)

Clear a good-sized space in the middle of the room for this skipping and marching game. The players take partners and line up facing each other in two equal rows. As everyone starts singing the well-known song that begins 'The Grand Old Duke of York', the pair at the top of the line join hands and skip with a running side-step down the middle of the rows and back again. When they return to their places at the top of the line, they split and march down behind their lines to the other end. When they reach the bottom, they face each other and continue singing, while the pair that are now at the top of the line join hands and skip down the middle as before. The game is completed when everybody has had a turn.

Here are the words of the song in case you don't know them:

> O the Grand Old Duke of York,
> He had ten thousand men,
> He marched them up to the top of the hill,
> And he marched them down again.
> And when they were up, they were up,
> And when they were down, they were down,
> And when they were only half-way up,
> They were neither up nor down!

Here We Go Round the Mulberry Bush *

Number: any number   *Age:* 4–8   *Time:* as many rounds as you care to make it   *Adult supervision:* leading in singing and calling topics to be mimed

This is a simple dancing and singing game well suited for parties with younger children. Get them to join hands and dance round in a circle while they sing:

> Here we go round the mulberry bush,
> The mulberry bush, the mulberry bush,
> Here we go round the mulberry bush,
> On a cold and frosty morning.

They then stand still and mime as they sing:

> This is the way to clap our hands,
> Clap our hands, clap our hands,
> This is the way we clap our hands,
> On a cold and frosty morning.

They form the circle once more and dance round singing the first verse. Then comes the second mime, which can be anything from 'brush our teeth' to 'wash the car', following the same pattern as the second verse. The game can continue for as long as you, your imagination and the children's energy will allow.

Musical Posture *

Number: any number   *Age:* 4 upwards   *Time:* up to 5 minutes, longer with a lot of players   *Adult supervision:* controlling music and judging players   (*Equipment:* source of music and one book for each player)

Here's a game of skill and poise to raise howls of delight and frustration. Everyone is given a book which they must balance on the head while walking round the room as the music plays. When the music stops all the players must stop too, go down on one knee, raise both hands in the air and stand up again *without dropping* the book. Give the instructions when the players should move, and don't keep younger players too long in any awkward position. Any child who drops a book, drops out of the game. The music starts again and the next round follows as before. The last remaining player is the winner.

Grand Chain *

Number: any even number   *Age:* 5 upwards   *Time:* up to 5 minutes   *Adult supervision:* controlling music   (*Equipment:* source of music and a balloon for each player)

Players divide into pairs and line up around the room. Each player is given a blown-up balloon which has to be held between the knees. When the music begins the players parade around the room in a grand chain trying to keep in time to the beat without dropping the balloons. Anyone who loses their balloon, either by dropping it or bursting it, leaves the Grand Chain along with their partner. The last pair left parading with their balloons wedged between their knees are the winners.

London Bridge

Number of players: 8 or more   *Age:* 5–8   *Time:* 5 minutes or longer   *Adult supervision:* leading singing and possibly forming the arch

The rules for this traditional old favourite are just the same as those for *Oranges and Lemons*, all that is different are the words sung to it. Either two adults or the two tallest players form London Bridge by joining hands and making an arch of their arms under which all the others march in a line, holding each other's waists and singing:

> London Bridge is falling down,
> Falling down, falling down,
> London Bridge is falling down,
> My Fair Lady!

On the word 'Lady!' the 'bridge' drops its arms and traps the player passing through. The players forming the bridge then swing their captive to and fro singing:

> Off to prison you must go,
> You must go, you must go,
> Off to prison you must go,
> My Fair Lady!

The player who has been caught goes and stands behind one side of the bridge, while the game continues and the song is repeated. The captured players divide themselves equally between the two sides of the bridge and at the end of the game, when all have been caught, there is a tug of war when the bridge does eventually fall down!

Musical Slipper *

Number: 4 or more   *Age:* 5–8   *Time:* 3–5 minutes   *Adult supervision:* controlling the music   (*Equipment:* source of music and a slipper)

Everyone sits in a tight circle on the floor, and a slipper is given to one of the players. The music starts and the slipper is passed round the circle from player to player as fast as possible and without stopping. Stop the music suddenly and see who is holding the slipper. That player drops out and the circle closes up to fill the empty space. The music starts again and the slipper passes from hand to hand faster than ever until the music stops again. One by one the players leave the circle until only one is left. That player is the winner, whose prize is replacing the slipper where it belongs!

Musical Numbers *

Number: 8 or more   *Age:* 5–8   *Time:* 5 minutes or longer, depending on number of players   *Adult supervision:* controlling music and judging players   (*Equipment:* source of music)

This game works just as well with a large party as with only eight players. In fact, the more there are to join in, the more fun everyone will have.

The music starts the game and the players dance round the room on their own; dancing in pairs or groups is not allowed, so keep an eye on those trying to cheat. The moment the music stops, call out a number to indicate the size of groups which the players must form. If you call 'five', for example, they have to rush to form groups of five. Call 'three', and they form groups of three. In calling your numbers, though, choose those that will always leave one or more players outside a group. The group must form circles with the right number of players and those not in a circle drop out before the music continues for the next round.

The game continues until only two players are left in the game and they become the two winners.

Musical Hats *

Number: 4 or more   *Age:* 4 upwards   *Time:* 2–5 minutes depending on number of players   *Adult supervision:* controlling music and judging players   (*Equipment:* source of music, paper hats)

The players sit in a circle. All but one are given paper hats. The moment the music starts they pass round the hats. When it stops all those with hats place them on their heads. The player left without a hat to wear leaves the circle, and takes one hat with him. The game continues until only one player is left, and he or she is the winner.

RACING GAMES

Waiter! Waiter! *

Number: 10 or more (even numbers) *Age:* 5 upwards
Time: 2–5 minutes *Adult supervision:* starting and judging
(*Equipment:* 2 plates, 2 ping pong balls)

Arrange the players into two equal teams and line them up with a good distance between each player. Give the first player in each team a plate with a ping pong ball on it. At the word 'Go!', both players run in and out down their team lines to the end and back again, saying to each player in their team, 'Here is your order, madam (sir).' When the 'waiter' returns to his position, the plate and ping pong ball are handed to the second player who runs down the line just as the first one did, weaving in and out and serving orders as before. Any player who drops the ping pong ball must return to the starting point to begin again. The first team to complete the waiters' run with all its players is the winner.

Thimble Race *

Number: any even number above 8 *Age:* 6 upwards *Time:* 1–2 minutes *Adult supervision:* starting and judging (*Equipment:* 2 thimbles and a straw for each player)

The players form two equal teams and stand in line, each player holding a straw in his or her mouth. The leaders of the teams are each given a thimble which is placed over the end of their straws. When the game starts, the first player in each team turns to the next player and passes the thimble from the end of one straw to the end of the second player's straw *without* using their hands. The second player then turns and passes the thimble to the third player, and so on down the line. The first team to pass its thimble from one end to the other wins. If the thimble is dropped (and it will be by both teams more than once), it must be returned to the leader to begin all over again!

Back to Front Race *

Number: any even number above 8   *Age:* 6 upwards   *Time:* 2–3
minutes   *Adult supervision:* starting and judging for fair play
(*Equipment:* 4 saucers and 24 objects)

The players divide into two teams and stand sideways on in line for this
exciting and challenging game. The leaders of the teams have at their
feet two saucers – one empty, the other filled with a dozen (or more) small
objects. (These can be used in other games, so a collection of fruit, sweets,
small toys, wooden bricks is worth having ready before the party begins.)
　　On the word 'Go!', the leader picks up one object at a time and passes
it down the line of players. When the object reaches the last player, it is
passed back up to the leader, only this time it has to be passed behind the
players' backs! While the game is in progress, then, objects are being
passed up and down the line at front and back and every player will be
passing two objects at the same time.
　　When the leaders receive the objects passed back to them, they must
place them in the empty saucer, keeping a check on the number
received. When the last one goes into the saucer, the leader shouts
'Finished'. The first team to do this wins.
　　If there are at least twice as many objects as there are players in a
team, this will keep everyone busy during the game!

Potato Race *

Number: 2 or more   *Age:* 5–9   *Time:* 1–2 minutes   *Adult
supervision:* starting and judging the finish   (*Equipment:* a
teaspoon and potato for each player)

Give each player a strong teaspoon (plastic ones will break under the
weight of the potatoes) and a potato, which should all be about the same
size for fair play. The players line up with their potatoes held in their
spoons. On the word 'Go!' they set off, balancing their potatoes against
accidents but trying to run faster than the other players. Players may not
touch the potatoes with their hands, but they are allowed to hold the
spoon with two hands, provided they only hold the handle. If a potato
falls to the ground it can be picked up, provided that the player uses his
spoon; if he touches the potato by hand at any time he must drop out of
the game.
　　The first player across the finishing line with the potato on the
spoon is the winner of a packet of potato crisps – what else?

Drop the Lot *

Number: any even number above 8   *Age:* 4 upwards   *Time:* 3–5 minutes   *Adult supervision:* starting and judging   (*Equipment:* 12 or more empty matchboxes)

The players form two teams and stand in line behind their leaders. Six or more empty matchboxes are placed on the ground in front of each leader. On the word 'Go!' the two leaders pick up the matchboxes in front of them and drop them from not lower than knee height at the feet of the players standing behind them. These players must frantically gather the boxes once more, turn round and drop them at the feet of the next player, and so on. When the boxes reach the last player in each line, he or she gathers them up, runs to the front of the line and drops them in front of the leader to begin the second round. This sequence continues until the original leader becomes the last player in each team. The leaders in their turn pick up the matchboxes and dash to the head of the line where the matchboxes are dropped at the front of the team with the triumphant cry of 'Finished!'. The first team to do this is the winner.

If playing with six matchboxes seems too easy, try doing it with eight!

Balloon Sweeping *

Number: 6 or more   *Age:* 5 upwards   *Time:* 3 to 5 minutes according to the number in each team   *Adult supervision:* starting, judging and keeping an eye on the furniture (*Equipment:* two brooms, two inflated balloons and some spares (uninflated) in case of accidents)

Before starting this game have a final check for any fragile or vulnerable furniture or ornaments that might be at risk with children chasing balloons with brooms! Form two teams and line them up at one end of the room. Place two chairs as markers at the opposite end, with enough clearance from the wall to allow players to pass behind them. Give a broom to the first player in each team and put the two balloons on the floor in front of them. At the word 'Go!' both players must sweep their balloons to the end of the room, round the chairs and back up to their teams, where the broom is handed to the second player who repeats the circuit before passing the broom to the next member of the team. The first team to get the last player back with the balloon is the winner. If either balloon bursts another is available, but this has to be blown up and tied before the sweeping can continue!

Marbles Race *

Number: any even number   *Age:* 5 upwards   *Time:* 2–3 minutes   *Adult supervision:* judging   (*Equipment:* 10 marbles and 2 paper plates)

Two teams are formed and stand in line behind their leader. Each leader is given a paper plate on which are rolling five marbles. On the word 'Go!' the leaders lift the plates above their heads and pass them backwards to the second players, who pass them backwards over their heads to the players standing behind, and so on down the line. Any marble dropped must be picked up by the player who dropped it and put back on the plate before it can be passed on down the line. When the last player in each team receives the plate, he or she runs to the front of the line to begin the second circuit. The game continues like this until the original leader is at the back of the line and receives the plate of marbles. He or she runs to the front and shouts 'Finished!'. The first team to complete the course with all the marbles is the winner.

Ankle Race *

Number: 2 or more   *Age:* 5 upwards   *Time:* 1–3 minutes
Adult supervision: judging and checking for cheating

The *Ankle Race* will appeal to energetic children of almost any age, though children over fifty should think twice before having a go!

The players line up on the starting line and get into the racing position, bending forward with a hand on each ankle. On the word 'Go!' they set off down the course racing as fast as they can, holding their ankles all the time. Any player who lets go of an ankle, even for a moment, or who trips and falls, must return to the starting point and begin all over again. The first player over the finishing line is the winner.

Pick and Cup Race *

Number: 10 or more   *Age:* 4 upwards   *Time:* 1–2 minutes
Adult supervision: judging   (*Equipment:* a number of small
unbreakable items, eg. fruit, balls of wool, small toys, wooden
bricks, etc.)

Divide the players into two teams and sit them on the floor facing each
other about one metre (three feet) apart. Go down the lines naming the
players alternately Pick or Cup, but starting and ending with a Pick. The
Cups sit with their hands cupped and held out to receive the items
dropped into them by the Picks.

   Place the same number of articles (at least ten) in a pile at the head of
each line. These should be small, unbreakable objects and, for the sake of
fair play, there should be similar objects in each pile.

   When both teams are ready, give the word to start. The player at the
head of each team picks up one of the objects and places it in the Cup
sitting next to him. The next Pick quickly lifts it out and drops it into the
next Cup down the line. And so the objects pass down the lines from Cup
to Pick to Cup and so on, until the last Pick takes them from the Cup next
to him and places them in a pile at his end.

   The first player may pass items down the line as quickly as he or she
likes, the aim of the game being to transfer all the objects from one end of
the line to the other before the other team. Whichever team succeeds in
doing this is the winner.

Snail's Race *

Number: 2 or more   *Age:* 4 upwards   *Time:* up to 5 minutes
depending on the skill of the winner/loser   *Adult supervision:*
judging that all the players *are* moving

The *Snail's Race* is unlike any other sort of race. It's aim is not to be the
first across the finishing line, but the *last*!

   The players all line up at the start. Before giving them the word 'Go!'
make sure that they all understand the object of the game, that is to move
as slowly towards the finishing line as they can. This may sound easy,
but remind them that they *must keep moving*; anyone who actually stops
moving is eliminated from the game.

   Once the game starts keep an eye on each player, checking that there
is some sign of movement, no matter how small. The players will find

they need great concentration to follow the rules and yet stay behind the rest of the field. To avoid the race lasting too long keep the course fairly short, and don't necessarily wait for the last player to cross the line; as soon as it is clear that he or she is the winner, award a small prize and move on to the next game.

(You might find this a good game to play to quieten the children down after a more boisterous session, and before tea perhaps.)

Feather Race *

Number: 2 or more   *Age:* 5 upwards   *Time:* 1–3 minutes
Adult supervision: judging   (*Equipment:* a feather and paper plate per player)

This is what you might call a lightweight race! Give each player a plate with a feather sitting on it. Line the players up on the starting line, and on the word 'Go!' let them set off towards the finishing line as fast as their feathers will allow them.

Feathers may not be touched by hand and if one drifts off a plate and floats to the ground, that player has to go back to the finishing line to start all over again. So it's very much a case of more haste less speed! The first player to cross the finishing line with feather on plate is the winner.

Fish Pool *

Number: 18   *Age:* 6 upwards   *Time:* 5 minutes or more depending on the skill of the players   *Adult supervision:* starting and judging the finish   (*Equipment:* 3 fans (hardboard or similar materials are fine) and 18 fishes (cut 6 of each from 3 different coloured pieces of paper), chalk or string for marking)

You will need ample space (ie. a large hall or party room rather than a private home) for this game, which is popular with large parties in which a lot of players can take part.

Start by clearing the playing area, and mark a circle in the centre of the floor using your chalk or string. This represents the fish pool.

The players are divided into three teams of six and are given the fish (six to a team). They stand in line about 10 metres (30 feet) from the pool at 4.00 o'clock, 8.00 o'clock and noon, to give an even space between each team. The first player in each team is given a fan and on the word 'Go!' he or she must fan one of the team's fish into the pool. Practice will soon show that waving the fan behind the paper fish will flip it towards the circle. As soon as the fish lands in the pool, the player runs to the back of his team, giving the fan to the next player as he passes. The second player then fans another fish into the pool as before.

Any player who fans a fish out of the pool has to fan it in again before continuing. The team that first fans all its fish into the pool is the winner.

(The number of players can be increased, or possibly decreased, providing there are the same number in each team, though it isn't practical to have more than three players trying to fan fish into the pool at the same time!)

Doll Dressing Race *

Number: any even number above 4   *Age:* 5 and upwards   *Time:* 2–5 minutes   *Adult supervision:* judging   (*Equipment:* dolls with the same number of clothes, one doll per team of 2)

Teams in this game consist of pairs, ideally one boy and one girl. Each pair is given a doll with a certain number of clothes to put on it. The first pair to dress their doll wins, all of which sounds rather easy and boring until you tell the players that the pairs may use only *one hand each*. Each player must have the other hand held firmly behind his or her back! For this reason it's as well not to have too many difficult clothes for the dolls to wear.

Burst the Bag Race *

Number: any even number above 6   *Age:* 6 upwards
Time: 1–3 minutes depending on the number of players   *Adult supervision:* judging   (*Equipment:* a paper bag per player)

The players divide into two teams and line up at one end of the room. At the other end are two equal piles of paper bags. On the word 'Go!' the first player in each team dashes to the other end, takes a paper bag from one of the piles and blows this up as fast as possible. Then with a mighty blow the bag is burst with a deafening 'Pop!', and the player rushes back to the team to touch the second player who hurtles down the track to pop the second bag. The moment that's done, the second player runs back and touches the third player who sets off to burst the next bag, and so on. The first team to burst all its paper bags is the winner.

(Remember that if you have animals in the house they may be frightened by the sound of the bursting bags. Comfort any cats or dogs, or better still have them away out of earshot during this game.)

Dressing-Up Race *

Number: 2 or more   *Age:* 5 upwards   *Time:* 3–5 minutes
Adult supervision: judging and watching out for possible trips with oversize shoes or long trousers   (*Equipment:* plenty of dressing-up clothes)

Children who enjoy racing and children who enjoy dressing up will love this game. Line up all the players on the starting line and place a pile of clothes for each one at the other end of the room. What you put in the pile depends on what you have available, the number of players and how old they are. Try to make the piles fairly even and include any jackets, large shoes, scarves and adult coats that you can spare – though keep your latest model outfit well out of harm's way! The more layers you can offer, the more fun the game will be.

On the word 'Go!' the players dash towards their pile of clothes and put on one item. Once this is done, they have to dash back to the starting line (touching a chair perhaps) and then run back down to the pile of clothes to put on another article. They have to keep running backwards and forwards in this way until all the clothes have been put on and they are back at the starting line. The first player to do this wins the game.

TALKING GAMES

I Packed My Bag *

Number: any number   *Age:* 6 upwards   *Time:* 3–5 minutes
Adult supervision: keeping check on contents of bag

This is a well-known memory game in which the players have to remember an ever-increasing list of items. The game starts with one player saying, for example: 'I packed my bag and in it I put my pyjamas.' The second player then repeats the sentence and adds another item, so: 'I packed my bag and in it I put my pyjamas and my teddy bear.' The third player does likewise: 'I packed my bag and in it I put my pyjamas, my teddy bear and my dressing-gown.' And so the bag passes round the group with each player repeating the contents that have already been put inside and adding one extra item. As the list of contents grows, the more difficult it is to remember them all and sooner or later one will be forgotten. The player who leaves out one of the items drops out of the game and helps judge the others. In the same way any player who includes a wrong item, or who gets one in the wrong order, leaves the game too. The last player left packing the bag in the right order wins the game.

Secrets

Number: any number   *Age:* 6 upwards   *Time:* 1–2 minutes a round   *Adult supervision:* making sure the secret is *whispered*

Everyone loves secrets and this game is popular with all age groups. The players sit in a circle and the first one whispers a secret into the ear of the player to the left. The secret is passed round the circle in this way, with one player whispering to another until the secret gets back to the player who started it. This player repeats the whisper out loud and then tells everyone the original secret. The two are usually wildly different. After this another player passes round a secret, and the game continues until everyone has had a go.

The Judge ^

Number: any even number plus a judge   *Age:* 5 upwards
Time: 3–5 minutes   *Adult supervision:* umpiring game to see
that the rules are followed

One player starts as the Judge while the others pair up and sit on the
floor. The Judge marches up and down the room, suddenly turns to one
pair and asks one of them a question. However, it is the *other player* who
must give the answer. Any player who speaks when he is spoken to, or
who doesn't speak when his partner is asked a question, has to leave the
game with his partner; so players have to keep on their toes.

   Clever judges can make the game great fun by asking players questions they are bursting to answer, in the hope of catching them out.
Sometimes an adult makes the best judge, but if the children are old
enough they can have great fun making up the questions themselves.

Backward Spelling *

Number: any number   *Age:* 8 upwards   *Time:* 3–5 minutes
Adult supervision: suggesting words and checking on spelling

Make a list beforehand of words that are moderately easy to spell. Sit all
the players in a line or circle and give a word to the first one. That player
must then spell it backwards in a set time (say 10–15 seconds). If the
player is successful, pass on to the next one. If a player fails, though, he
or she loses one 'life'. Play the game for five or six rounds, giving each
player in each round a word of about the same difficulty. The player who
has lost the fewest number of lives at the end of the game is the winner.

What Are We Shouting? *

Number: any number   *Age:* 8 upwards   *Time:* 5 minutes
Adult supervision: judging and possibly helping with proverbs
and phrases

The players form two teams, one of which gathers together in a corner or
out of the room to decide on a well-known phrase or proverb (if a team
has difficulty, have a shortlist of suitable ones to help them along).

Suppose the team decides on 'Too many cooks spoil the broth', they count the number of words, find there are six and divide them between team members. If there are six in the team, each gets one word. If there are more than six then two or more players will have to share words. If there are less than six players, they will have to choose another phrase with the right number of words to suit the team size. When it's been agreed which players have which words, they go to the other team and after a count of three all shout their words at the same time. The other team may ask to hear the words shouted three times if they wish, but after that they have to make a guess. If a team cannot guess it correctly, the other team can go back to its corner to choose another phrase or proverb. If it is successful, though, it then has a chance to shout a proverb or phrase of its own.

Common sayings, film and television titles, the titles of stories and songs will all make suitable subjects for group shouting.

Poison Letters *

Number: any number   *Age:* 7 upwards   *Time:* 5 minutes
Adult supervision: checking on words for the 'poison letter'

In each round of this game, one letter of the alphabet is 'poison' and words containing it may not be used in answers. Players have to think of words that answer the question put to them, but which avoid the poison letter.

The leader of the game starts with the formula: 'The Great Panjandrum does not like P. What shall we give him to eat?' In answer to this the other players may reply 'cabbage', 'bread', 'honey', 'beef' or 'ice cream', but they must not use words containing P like 'potato', 'spinach' and 'apples'. Anyone who makes the mistake of using the poison letter drops out, and the game continues until only one player is left in the group. That player is the winner and has the chance to name the poison letter in the next round.

Donkey *

Number: any number   *Age:* 8 upwards   *Time:* 2–5 minutes a round   *Adult supervision:* guarding the dictionary in case of disputes   (*Equipment:* a dictionary (preferably a children's one))

The object of this popular old spelling game is to be the last player to become a DONKEY, and to do that you have to avoid being the player to complete the spelling of the words in the game.

One player starts the ball rolling by naming a letter. The next player follows with a second letter which really forms part of a word. The third player adds a third letter (which might in fact form a three-letter word like THE, except that three-letter words don't count in this game!). The other players add letters until one is either forced to end a word by mistake, or because he or she can't think of a way of continuing. Any player who ends a word loses a life and collects the letter D, the first in the word DONKEY. After losing six lives and becoming a DONKEY, that player drops out. The last left in the game is the winner.

Suppose the first player says C thinking of 'CRANE'

> the second adds H thinking of CHAIR
> the third adds A thinking of Chair also
> the fourth adds R thinking of CHART
> the fifth adds G thinking of CHARGE

Now the sixth could add I to lead the word towards CHARGING, but in this case that idea doesn't come to him and for lack of any other ideas he adds E making CHARGE and so completing the word. He loses one life and gets a D.

If a player suspects that another has added a letter to avoid ending a word but without having a real word in mind, he can challenge the previous player. If it is proved (usually through the dictionary) that the player either didn't have a word at all, or was trying to spell that word incorrectly, that player loses a life. But if there really was such a word, then it's the challenger who loses a life.

The last player to be DONKEY has the chance to start the next word in the next game.

The Old Oak Chest *

Number: any number   *Age:* 7 upwards   *Time:* 5 minutes
Adult supervision: introducing the game and checking on items
in the chest

If you want a quiet game to amuse children while they are digesting tea,
this will certainly fit the bill with older age groups.

Sit the players on the floor and start the game by saying: 'Up in the
attic there's an old oak chest and in that chest there's a big axe' (or
anything beginning with A). The next player now picks up the line and
says: 'Up in the attic there's an old oak chest and in that chest there's a
big anvil' (or anything else beginning with A). Everyone in turn repeats
the sentence adding another item beginning with A until the leader's
turn comes round again. Now the items have to start with the letter B,
and so on through the alphabet (though X and Z can be left out since
words beginning with these letters are not very common in English.)

Players may not repeat words already used by others, and any player
who fails to think of an item beginning with the right letter must drop
out of the game. The last player left in the game is the winner.

I Spy

Number: any number   *Age:* 4 upwards   *Time:* as long as the
players wish   *Adult supervision:* only necessary to check that
what is spied is actually in view

Of all the Talking Games this is the best known and most popular. You
can play it anywhere, with any number and for as long as you like. It tests
powers of observation and keeps everyone guessing.

One player starts the game as the Spy, saying to the others: 'I spy
with my little eye something beginning with B (or C, or D, or any other
letter of the alphabet). The others then take it in turn to guess what the
Spy has spied. It might be a book, or a bench, or a brick, or a bunny, or a
basket or any number of things beginning with B. Whatever it is, though,
it must be in view at the time of spying. The player who is the first to
guess correctly what the Spy spied becomes the Spy in the next round.

The Minister's Cat

Number: any number *Age:* 8 upwards (younger children might
enjoy this with a little help) *Time:* 5 minutes *Adult
supervision:* helping younger players with useful hints

This is another old favourite with players who like alphabet games. It's
quiet and well suited to that period immediately after tea.

The aim of the game is to describe the minister's cat with adjectives
that begin with the first letter of the alphabet and then all the others one
by one. The first player might begin by saying: 'The minister's cat is an
aged cat.' The second might say: 'The minister's cat is an angry cat.' The
third might say: 'The minister's cat is an agile cat.' And the game
continues round the group until every player has thought of an adjective
beginning with A to describe the cat. Then comes B with 'bad', 'beauti-
ful', 'beastly', 'brave', and lots of other words.

Some letters will be easier than others (and X and Z are best left out
altogether). Younger players might prefer to play a simplified form in
which each player thinks of an adjective beginning with a different letter
of the alphabet. The first starts with A, the second has B and so on. This
will make the game easier and quicker. If they want to play the full
version, give a few gentle hints to players who get stuck. 'What is a cat
when it's cross?' for example.

Don't Stop Talking

Number: any number *Age:* 4 upwards *Time:* 30 seconds per
player *Adult supervision:* time keeping (*Equipment:* a clock
or watch with a second hand, or a kitchen timer)

Children who enjoy telling stories will certainly enjoy this game, as will
those who can't stop talking!

The first player starts telling a story and for thirty seconds must talk
non-stop. When the time is up, the story passes to the next player on the
left who must continue from where the story left off, again talking for
thirty seconds without stopping. The story progresses round the group
in this way, with each player contributing thirty seconds of constant
chatter, until it comes to the last player who has to finish the story in the
same thirty seconds!

There are no winners or losers in this game, but the players will hear
some very odd stories!

Twenty Questions

Number: any number   *Age:* 8 upwards   *Time:* 3–5 minutes
Adult supervision: counting 20 questions

Twenty Questions is based on the popular radio programme which has made it one of the most well-known word games in the world. Players take it in turns to think of objects, one each, which the others have to try and guess in just twenty questions. Only questions calling for 'Yes' or 'No' answers are allowed. The player who has thought of a secret object must answer each question truthfully, but it is up to the other players to piece the answers together and come up with the right answer.

   Any objects can be chosen: household objects, animals, plants, types of transport, anything that the other children might have heard of and know about. If after the twenty questions are up, no one has guessed the secret object, the player who thought of it can have another go. On the other hand, a player who guesses correctly has a chance to think of another object and face twenty questions from the others.

What's My Name? *

Number: any number   *Age:* 7 upwards   *Time:* 5 minutes
Adult supervision: checking on suitability of names and judging answers to questions made by 'It'

One of the players is chosen as 'It', and leaves the room while the others decide on who 'It' is going to be. 'It' can be anyone from Superman or Dr Who to Prince Philip or the Princess of Wales. All that matters is that 'It's' identity should be well known to everyone playing the game.

   When the players have decided who 'It' is going to be, 'It' is brought back into the room. 'It' then has three questions to put to every player, all of them calling for 'Yes', 'No', or 'I don't know' answers, questions like 'Am I alive?', 'Am I a person in a story?', 'Am I a woman?'. At the end of the questions 'It' has to decide who 'It' is. If the guess is right, 'It' wins a small prize. If not, no prize is awarded. Either way, another player becomes 'It' and leaves the room for the next round.

Sausages

Number: any number   *Age:* 5 upwards   *Time:* 3–5 minutes
Adult supervision: judging and eliminating players

This is one of those silly games that is great fun to play when everyone is in the party mood and having a good time. It's not the best game to start a party with!

A victim is chosen from among the players and the others fire questions at him or her. These should be personal questions about school, holidays, favourite activities, names of teachers, anything to do with the victim, in fact. To every question the victim has the same answer: 'Sausages'. So the game goes something like this: *Q.* 'What's your favourite colour?' *A.* 'Sausages.' *Q.* 'What do you call your bike?' *A.* 'Sausages.' The point is that the victim has to keep a perfectly straight face throughout the game, however ridiculous the answer sounds. Any smile, any giggle, any rolling on the floor in helpless fits of laughter, and the victim loses and gives way to another victim.

Of course, there is nothing to prevent the other players from laughing and giggling as much as they like – that just makes it all the more difficult for the victim!

I Want a Rhyme

Number: 4 or more   *Age:* 5 upwards   *Time:* 5 minutes or longer   *Adult supervision:* only to check on suitability of words chosen for rhyming

One of the players starts as the leader and stands up in front of the others (who are sitting down) to say:

> 'I want a rhyme
> In jolly quick time,
> And the word I choose is: "MAT"

The word doesn't have to be MAT, it can be any word that has a lot of other words that rhyme with it, words like: HID, SEAT, COAL, STABLE, FARM, and so on. (Words that have very few rhymes should be discouraged; try suggesting others if they crop up because they only drag the game out as the children rack their brains trying to find a rhyme.)

After the leader has given a word, the other players give rhyming words in order, one after the other. So with MAT you might get: CAT,

SAT, FLAT, HAT, CHAT, FAT, THAT, BAT and SLAT, with the words going round and round the group until one player fails to think of a rhyme and has to drop out. Players are allowed a count of 1 to 10 before they are out. The others try to keep going, thinking of rhymes that haven't already been used. In the end only one player will be left, though, and that player becomes the leader for the next round and the next rhyme.

ACTING GAMES

Charades

Number: any number   *Age:* 6 upwards   *Time:* at least 4 minutes to every word   *Adult supervision:* advising on words to be acted

This is one of the oldest and most popular party games with players of all ages. There are different variations depending on the age of the participants, but this children's version loses none of the fun and excitement of adult versions.

The players divide into two teams and take it in turns to think of words to act out in front of the other team. They should choose two-syllable words that can be divided easily into two parts (here a little adult advice might be handy, so have a list of suitable words ready). A few suggestions are: quicksand, seaside, moonbeam, roundhead, football, grandfather and X-ray.

After choosing its word, a team must decide on three short scenes which they can act to help the members of the other team guess what their word is. The first scene gives the first part of the word, the second scene gives the second part and the third scene gives the whole word.

Let's suppose that a team has settled on ARMCHAIR. They need to present a first scene that illustrates the first part of the word – 'arm'. So they might act out a little scene in which sportsmen are using their arms. This could be a training session, perhaps, with cricketers standing still except for moving their bowling arms, weight-lifters lifting with their arms and tennis players moving their arms as though hitting the ball. There could even be one actor feeling the muscles in his arm. As long as all the team concentrate on 'arm', the message should sink in. In the second scene they have to act the second part of the word, 'chair'. Here they could act a scene in which everyone is looking for a chair for an important person who has to remain standing until finally a chair is produced (this isn't a real chair, of course, its arrival and use have to be acted). In the last scene the team have to illustrate the whole word. To do this they might act a scene in which a removal firm carries a big heavy armchair into a new house, the owner lovingly dusts it and puffs the cushions before sinking back into it exhausted.

Allow each team at least four minutes to plan and act out their three scenes, and give any help and encouragement they need. Some children might feel shy about acting at first, but after one round they'll become more confident. Encourage them to prepare their charades well, because these are always the most enjoyable to watch – and the most difficult to guess.

Act the Word

Number: any number   Age: 8 upwards   Time: 2–3 minutes per word   Adult supervision: advising on words (when required)

Here's a game which tests the imagination and amuses players from 8 to 80, though bright younger children can get a lot of fun from playing with simpler words too.

One player leaves the room while the others choose their 'acting' word, such as 'happily', 'bravely', 'quickly', 'angrily', 'carelessly'. The player who has left the room then comes in again and has to guess the chosen word. To get some clues he or she can ask any of the other players to perform a certain task in the manner of the secret word. They can read a book, drive a car, swat a fly, put on a coat or perform any other action, but they must do it in the way described by the secret word.

As soon as the player has guessed the word, another player leaves the room and the second word is chosen. Words shouldn't be too difficult because everyone likes to guess words if they possibly can, and it's a good idea to let everyone have a go. So keep the game moving by choosing suitable words and giving helpful hints if a player looks hopelessly stuck.

Dumb Show

Number: any number   *Age:* 5 upwards   *Time:* 5 minutes
Adult supervision: suggesting topics for miming (if needed)

In this acting game the audience have almost as much fun as the actors. Divide the players into two teams, one to be the audience, one the actors. The actors leave the room while the audience decide on an activity for them to act out. This should be a common, everyday activity but one which is fairly difficult to act, one like filling the car with petrol, or plugging in a vacuum cleaner and cleaning the carpet. When the audience have decided on their activity, one of the actors is called into the room and told what the activity is. A second actor then comes in and the first mimes the activity to him. Then the third actor comes in and the second repeats the mime. The third repeats to the fourth, and so on throughout the group until the last actor mimes the activity and then says what he thinks it is. By now it's likely to have moved some way from filling the car with petrol or vacuuming the carpet!

When the audience have recovered from their hysterics, they go out of the room while the new audience decide on an activity for them.

Dumb Crambo

Number: any number   *Age:* 7 upwards   *Time:* 2–3 minutes per mime   *Adult supervision:* suggesting suitable words (when needed)

Two teams are formed and one leaves the room while the other chooses a *verb* – talk, dance, play, jump, run, look, for example. Once the verb is chosen the other team comes back into the room and is told a word that *rhymes* with the secret verb.

If the team in the room had chosen 'look', the other team might be told that the secret verb rhymes with 'took'. That team must now try to guess the secret verb and act it out in dumb-show. If the audience see them all holding one hand in front of them as though grasping a handle, and stirring inside a pot with the other, they hiss because the secret verb isn't 'cook', which the acting team clearly think it is. They have to try again. Now they are seen holding fishing lines and catching fish. Again the audience hiss because the secret verb isn't 'hook' either. Finally the acting team hold their hands to their foreheads and peer into the dis-

tance. A loud cheer goes up from the audience because the actors have at
last guessed that the secret verb is 'look'.

When the secret verb has been guessed, the teams change places for
the next game.

Simon Says *

Number: any number   *Age:* 4 upwards   *Time:* 3–5 minutes
Adult supervision: judging actions of players

Simon Says (O'Grady Says and many other titles) is the most popular of
all mimicking games. It is great fun to play at any age and can be made as
easy or difficult as the party calls for.

One of the players is chosen as the leader, Simon, and the others
spread themselves out around the room in front of him. Everything
Simon says must be obeyed, *provided that the order begins with the
words 'Simon says'*. Any order that *doesn't begin* with 'Simon says' must
be ignored.

Simon might begin by saying: 'Simon says hands on heads' at which
everyone must put their hands on their heads. 'Simon says stand on one
foot' and everyone stands on one foot. But with the next order 'Raise
right hands', every hand must stay on the head, because the order didn't
begin with 'Simon says'. Any player who raises a right hand has to drop
out.

Simon can make the players run on the spot, close their eyes, hold
an ear, sit on the floor, lie on their backs or do any other action, but the
players must have their ears open all the time waiting for the trick orders
that leave out the important words 'Simon says'. The last player left in
the game wins.

Dumb Nursery Rhymes

Number: any number   *Age:* 5 upwards   *Time:* 2–3 minutes per
act   *Adult supervision:* only to suggest suitable nursery rhymes
(if necessary)

Players who enjoy miming will adore this game, so divide the party into
small groups of three or four to allow everyone to have a fair share of the

action. One group leaves the room to select a nursery rhyme and to work out how they should mime it. Once they have decided, they come back into the room and perform their mime. They may use any props or costumes they like (so have a few suitable items waiting outside the door – simple things like hats, coats, sticks and perhaps a sheet that could be used as a cloak or long dress are all that is needed), but they must not utter a word during the performance. Anyone caught talking has to leave the stage!

When the other team have guessed the title of the nursery rhyme, it's their turn to go outside and select another for their mime.

Noah's Ark

Number: 7 or more   Age: 5–8   Time: 5 minutes   Adult supervision: only to make sure everyone knows what they are meant to be doing

The player chosen as Noah stands at one end of the room at the entrance to the Ark. The other players divide into pairs to enter the Ark 'two by two'. The players are two animals – one Mr . . . , the other Mrs . . . – so if they can pair off boy-girl, boy-girl, so much the better.

The Mr in each pair decides which animal he is going to be – a lion, a monkey, a fish, a horse, a dog, a cat, any animal he can imitate – and he begins making all this animal's movements and sounds. But he doesn't tell his Mrs what animal he is; she has to follow his movements as best she can.

When they are ready the animals go to Noah in their pairs, one pair at a time. The Mr animal asks Noah: 'Mr Noah, will you please let us into your Ark?' To which Noah replies: 'Of course I will, but what kind of animal are you?' Now it's the Mrs who has to reply, and her answer will depend on how good the Mr is at acting. If she gives the right answer, she and her partner go straight into the Ark and are saved from the flood. If she gets it wrong, they have to go back to the end of the line and start all over again. The game continues like this until all the animals are in the Ark.

Acting Clumps *

Number: any number above 6   *Age:* 6 upwards   *Time:* 5 minutes   *Adult supervision:* whispering words and judging the miming   (*Equipment:* list of words or actions for teams to act and guess)

Two teams are formed and they should be put as far away from each other as possible, preferably into separate rooms. An umpire sits mid-way between the two teams (two umpires might be necessary if two rooms are used) and holds a list of words or actions which each team must act and guess. These might be objects like: a cricket bat, a hair-dryer, a frying pan, a swing, an animal, a new hat, a tree. Or they might be actions like: driving a car, putting up a tent, eating spaghetti, putting on a pair of tight trousers, firing a gun, digging the garden, or swimming.

On the word 'Go' one player from each team runs to the umpire who whispers the same word or action to each player, keeping the list well out of sight. The players rush back to their teams and *without saying a word* mime the word or action. The other members of the team have to guess the word or action with no help from the actor. As soon as they have done this (and the umpire can judge when they are right), another member of the team runs to the umpire to collect the second word or action and then dashes back to mime this to the rest of the team. The first team to guess all the words or actions on the lists wins.

What Are We?

Number: any number   *Age:* 4–8   *Time:* 1–2 minutes per act

Younger children enjoy acting but may find more difficult games like *Charades* too much for them. With this game everyone can join in, and the guessing part is easy and great fun.

The children divide into two groups with a leader in each. One group sits on the floor as the audience for the first act, while the others go out of the room to decide what they will act. They have to choose the name of an animal or bird which is easy for everyone to imitate; cows, pigs, donkeys, elephants, tigers and lions, cats, cuckoos, would all be good examples. Once they've decided, the players return and act out the animal with full sound effects! Each member of the group acts the same animal, but you can be sure that even in a pride of lions there will be some very unusual creatures!

When one side has finished its act (and don't let them last for longer than twenty or thirty seconds), the others try to guess what the animal is. They then go out of the room to prepare an act of their own.

Destination Please?

Number: any number   *Age:* 7 upwards   *Time:* 2–3 minutes per act   *Adult supervision:* suggesting suitable destinations (if needed)

This game combines the skills of acting and spelling. Younger children might enjoy playing a simple version, that is one that uses destinations with only a few letters, but it is really a game better suited to older players.

Two teams are formed, and while one sits on the floor as the audience, the other goes out of the room to decide on a town or city to which they are travelling. When they return they must mime one action for each letter in the name of the town or city, and that action must begin with the letter they are miming. They can mime as a team or let each member mime a different letter. If a team choose Bristol, for example, they might mime: biting; rowing; injecting; stealing; typing; opening a door; and looking.

When all the mimes are completed, the audience have to guess the destination of the actors. If they want, they can ask for mimes to be repeated and the actors must repeat them exactly as they first performed them. Give the audience a time limit to guess the town or city. Then, whether they get the right answer or not, send them out to think of a destination of their own.

Poor Pussy *

Number: any even number   *Age:* 5 upwards   *Time:* 3–5 minutes   *Adult supervision:* judging and eliminating players

This is one of those daft games which is actually great fun to play, and surprisingly difficult to play well. It's an acting game that needs a lot of self-control on the part of one player and a lot of acting skill on the part of the others.

The players divide into two equal rows and stand face to face about 2 metres (6½ feet) apart. The first player goes to the player opposite, kneels down and says 'meow' three times! The other player must then stroke the head of the player kneeling down and say 'Poor pussy!' without smiling, giggling, laughing or falling over in helpless fits of mirth. If he can do this successfully, the roles change and he goes across to the next player, kneels down and says 'meow' three times. Anyone who can't keep a straight face drops out. The last player left in the game wins – sour puss!

Acting Proverbs

Number: any number   *Age:* 8 upwards   *Time:* 4 minutes per proverb   *Adult supervision:* advising on proverbs where necessary and providing helpful hints if needed

Divide the players into small groups of three or four and send one group out of the room to think of a well-known proverb that they can act out for the others to guess. The actors can use any props they want and can talk as much as they like, but they must act the whole proverb in one scene. As soon as a group has thought of a proverb, they return to the room and act it out in front of the others who must guess what it is. When one group has acted their proverb, they join the audience and the next group goes out.

It's as well to have a list of proverbs ready to help any groups who have problems deciding on one. Here are a few common ones which you might find useful:

> Too many cooks spoil the broth.
> Look before you leap.
> Don't count your chickens before they're hatched.
> A stitch in time saves nine.
> A rolling stone gathers no moss.
> People in glass houses shouldn't throw stones.
> Don't put all your eggs in one basket.
> Many hands make light work.

Please Pass

Number: any number *Age:* 4–8 *Time:* 2–5 minutes *Adult supervision:* only to make sure that objects passed can be moved and touched without any damage to life or limb *(Equipment:* a few everyday objects placed strategically round the room, with one or two unusual items included with them.)

This simple game can be great fun for players who enjoy using their acting talents and exercising their imagination. Before the game begins, perhaps even before the party begins, place a few everyday objects in the room, like: mustard pots, toothbrushes, shoe brushes, dusters, bottle-openers, and include with them a few unexpected things, like a hammer, a tent peg, or door-knob.

Sit all the players in a circle. The game begins with one of them miming an object. This might be a bathing-cap, a nail brush or a fork. Whatever it is, the player must be able to see it in the room, and must mime its use until one of the others collects the object and passes it to the player. The player who passes the object then has a go at miming another object, and so the game progresses until all the objects have been passed and, with luck, everyone has had a go at miming something. (A little diplomatic help might be needed to achieve the last part!)

PAPER AND PENCIL GAMES

Equipment: Pencils and paper are needed for all games in this section.

Kim's Game *

Number: any number *Age:* 7 upwards *Time* 5 minutes
Adult supervision: preparation of game and judging answers
(Equipment: a tray with a number of different objects)

As a game that tests powers of observation and memory, *Kim's Game* is hard to beat. It features in Rudyard Kipling's great novel of India, *Kim*, in which the hero acquires his skill as a secret agent by first playing this game.

Before the guests arrive, or while they are in another room, eating tea perhaps, arrange a collection of twenty or thirty objects, as different as possible, on a tray or table and cover them with a cloth. Try to find as many varied objects as you can, but alter the number to suit the age of the players. Younger children may be daunted by too many, so give them ten or a dozen; they will enjoy the game just as much.

When the players come into the room, give each a piece of paper and a pencil. Tell them they have thirty seconds to study the contents of the tray before it is covered. During that time they must only look at the objects to try and remember them, *nothing must be written*. Only when the tray has been covered again, may they start listing the objects from memory. Allow three minutes or longer depending on the number of objects on the tray and then collect in the papers, making sure they are all named. The player who has listed the most objects correctly is the winner. However, any objects included in the list that were *not* in fact on the tray cancel out one of the correct entries. (With younger players you may need to allow extra time for slow writers.)

Dotty Drawings

Number: any number   *Age:* any age   *Time:* 2–3 minutes
Adult supervision: setting game going and helping to judge drawings

Give each player a sheet of paper and a pencil and ask everyone to make six random dots on their papers. When these have been made (and check that everyone has made six dots), get the players to pass their sheets to the right, so that everyone ends up with someone else's sheet. Now comes the fun. Ask the players to use the random dots to draw some sort of picture by joining them to make an animal or person. This might be quite a challenge, but children will enjoy creating unusual animals and funny faces. When everyone has finished, hold up the pictures and let everyone join in the fun.

Jumbled Proverbs *

Number: any number   *Age:* 8 upwards   *Time:* 5–10 minutes
Adult supervision: providing proverbs and judging answers

Give each player a sheet of paper and a pencil and then read a list of
proverbs to them. In every case the proverb has been jumbled, and the
players have to unjumble the words and put them into the right order
before writing down the proverb as it should read. These are some
examples of proverbs you might include:

> Shines hay sun while the make.
> The horse bolted shut the stable-door after don't has.
> The brush worth is a hand in two bird the in.

It oughtn't to take you too long to work out that these are the
proverbs:

> Make hay while the sun shines.
> Don't shut the stable-door after the horse has bolted.
> A bird in the hand is worth two in the bush.

But children, especially those who may not know the proverbs well,
will enjoy puzzling over ten to fifteen of these, trying to unscramble
them. Obviously you should choose proverbs to suit the party, and if
you have played a proverb game earlier in the party, perhaps *Acting
Proverbs*, you might use some of these again to see how good the
children's memories are. The player with the most correct answers wins.

Heads and Tails *

Number: any number   *Age:* 8 upwards   *Time:* 5 minutes
Adult supervision: time keeping and judging answers

Players are given five minutes in which to write down as many words as
they can that begin and end with the same letter, words like: ewe, gag,
lull, says, dived, going, bomb. At the end of the game, one point is
awarded for each word and the player with the highest score wins.

Sounds Off *

Number: any number   *Age:* 6 upwards   *Time:* 3–5 minutes
Adult supervision: making noises and checking answers
(*Equipment:* objects with which to make various noises)

All the players are given paper and pencils, and seated somewhere where they can write and yet be within earshot of the door. Go out of the door and almost close it, leaving only a small opening. Have a tray waiting on the other side, but hidden from view, on which are a variety of objects with which to make a noise. Tell the players that they have to write down what they think the noise is after each one has been made; tell them, too, not to talk during the game in case they miss a noise. Then call out 'Number One' and make the first noise. After a short break, say 'Number Two' and make the second. Carry on for fifteen or twenty noises.

These are some of the noises you might make:

> Striking a match
> Winding a clock
> Sharpening a knife
> Using a piece of sandpaper on wood
> Opening a tin of fizzy drink
> Cutting paper with a pair of scissors

Constantinople *

Number: any number   *Age:* 7 upwards   *Time:* 10 minutes
Adult supervision: checking answers   (*Equipment:* a large sheet of paper and a marker pen)

Each player is given a paper and pencil. The leader writes a long word, for example CONSTANTINOPLE, on a large sheet of paper and places it in a position where every player can see. The players then have ten minutes in which to write down as many words that they can think of which are formed with the letters in the large word. Only letters appearing in the original word more than once may be used in the new words more than once, so in the case of Constantinople 'toot' would be allowed but 'sees' would not. No names are allowed either, so Stan, Tina and Connie may not be included in the list. The player with the longest list of words at the end of the time limit wins the game.

Find the Adjectives *

Number: any number   *Age:* 8 upwards   *Time:* 5 minutes
Adult supervision: selecting passage for game and judging
answers   (*Equipment:* a passage from a book or a newspaper)

Give each of the players a sheet of paper and a pencil. Then dictate a
short passage from a story or other suitable piece of prose, leaving out a
dozen of the adjectives. Every time you come to one of the adjectives to
be omitted, say 'blank'. After reading the passage through, give the
players a list of the adjectives you left out, but jumble up their order.
Then give them two or three minutes to put the adjectives in the right
'blanks' before giving the correct answers. The player who gets all, or
nearly all, the adjectives in the right place wins the game.

Word Power *

Number: any number   *Age:* 7 upwards   *Time:* 1 minute per
topic (longer if need be)   *Adult supervision:* only judging
answers (the idea is to free you for a moment))

If you need a trouble-shooter during a minor panic, this game can be a
godsend. If the cake won't come out of the tin, if the film projector blows
a bulb, if the conjurer remembers he's left something vital in the car, or if
Father Christmas arrives without his sack, you can play this game for a
couple of minutes until the problem is solved, and if need be you can
leave the children to it for a moment by themselves.

All you have to do is to sit them down, give each of them a sheet of
paper and a pencil, and tell them to list as many things as they can under
a particular heading. Tell them they have a minute (longer if you want).
Then give them a heading and set them off. The player with the longest
list is the winner.

Here are some topics that might make good general headings:

>Things that produce light
>Animals that only come out at night
>Names of trees
>Musical instruments
>Articles of clothing
>Television programmes
>Tools that cut through different materials.

Ten Pennies *

Number: any number   *Age:* 7 upwards   *Time:* 5 minutes
Adult supervision: hiding pennies and judging answers
(Equipment: 10 pennies)

All the players leave the room while you hide the ten pennies. Don't hide them completely. Try to hide them cleverly so that they can be seen only from one angle, for example, or need sharp eyes to spot them poking out from under picture frames or plants.

Call the players back when all the coins are in place and tell them to move round the room *in silence* looking for the coins. They mustn't touch them or tell their friends where the coins are. All they need do is write down where each is hidden. The first player to spot all ten wins or, if no player manages that, the one with the most coins on his or her list when time is up wins the game.

Consequences

Number: any number   *Age:* 7 upwards   *Time:* 5 minutes
Adult supervision: giving instructions during the game

This game is played with every member writing down certain pieces of information. After every piece of information, the player must fold over the top of the paper to cover what has been written, and pass the folded piece of paper to the player on the right. At the same time he or she receives another piece of folded paper from the player on the left. New information is added to each sheet, therefore, without any of the players knowing what has been written on it before. At the end of the game the pieces of paper are opened up and each one reveals a short story which is read aloud.

These are the eight pieces of information the players must write down:

1. An adjective describing a person (eg. Silly)
2. The name of a girl (eg. Snow White)
3. The word 'met' and an adjective that describes a person (eg. puny)
4. The name of a boy or man (eg. Batman)
5. The word 'at' and the name of a place (eg. Windsor Castle)
6. The words 'He said to her', and what he said (eg. 'Two coca colas please.')

7. The words 'She said to him', and what she said (eg. 'If you do, I'll call the police.')

8. The words 'And the consequence was', and what it was (eg. 'They lived happily ever after.')

If this particular story was read out loud at the end of the game, this is what it would sound like: 'Silly Snow White met puny Batman at Windsor Castle. He said to her, "Two coca colas, please." She said to him, "If you do, I'll call the police." And the consequence was they lived happily ever after.' When you play the game, you get as many different stories as there are players and they will all be very funny, especially if you play the game for several rounds to get everyone in the mood.

Letter Sentence

Number: any number   *Age:* 7 upwards   *Time:* 1 minute per round   *Adult supervision:* judging answers

Give all the players a sheet of paper and a pencil. One player is chosen to be leader for the first round and calls out four letters of the alphabet at random. The other players then try to write a four-word sentence, using words beginning with each of the letters in order. If the leader calls out 'S, D, B, N', one player might write the answer 'Sardines do behave naughtily', while another's answer might be 'Seventy dogs bark noisily.'

When everyone has written a sentence, read them out aloud – you might get some very funny ones. Then let another player be leader and work round the whole group, giving everyone a chance to call out the letters. (If you find that the sentences are written in less than a minute, cut the time down to keep the game lively and brisk.)

Picture Spotting *

Number: any number   *Age:* 5 upwards   *Time:* 6 minutes
Adult supervision: preparing checklist of items in pictures and judging answers   (*Equipment:* six large pictures taken from papers or magazines, and cardboard on which to mount them)

Like *Kim's Game*, this is a game of observation but this one is easier because players can write down the objects as they see them, the only problem is one of time; they have only one minute per picture. (With younger players you might find it better to remove this time limit and allow them, say, seven or eight minutes, as well as providing simpler pictures.)

The game calls for some preparation before the party. You will need to find six large pictures, full of detail. Photographs of street scenes, aerial photographs of cities, airports or docks, any photographs containing a good number of recognizable objects will be ideal. Mount each of these on a sheet of cardboard and arrange them around the party room before the game begins.

Give each player a sheet of paper and a pencil. Point to the pictures, which should be numbered or lettered in some way for identification, and explain that each player must write down as many things that he or she can see in each one. Only one example of each item need be given, you don't want lists of cars, for example; it's variety that counts. Tell the players how long they have for the game and then set them off. It's a good idea to have a checklist of your own of the items in each picture (though you can be sure that some sharp-eyed child will spot something you have missed). When time is up, read out the objects in each picture and see which child has the highest score. That one wins the game.

Blindfold Drawing

Number: any number   *Age*: 4 upwards   *Time*: 5 minutes
Adult supervision: blindfolding, giving instructions and judging pictures   (*Equipment*: blindfolds)

Sit all the players at tables and give each one a sheet of paper and a pencil. Now blindfold them all. When everyone is securely blindfolded, tell them to draw a picture of a house. When they think they have completed this task, ask them to add some hills behind the house. Then ask them to put a garden in front. After this, ask them to draw some clouds in the sky. Lastly, tell them to add a policeman in the garden.

When all the drawings are completed, tell the players to remove their blindfolds and let everyone have a good laugh at the results, most of which will be crazy!

Feel It *

Number: any number   *Age:* 6 upwards   *Time:* 3–5 minutes
Adult supervision: preparing objects and judging answers
(*Equipment:* a pillow-case with objects to go inside)

Before the party begins, put a number of objects into a pillow-case in preparation for this game. They should be as varied as you can make them. You might put in: a toggle from a duffle coat; a key; a matchbox; a thimble; a rubber; an orange; a piece of soap; a toy soldier; a toy car; a button; a coin; a pencil – any objects that are ready to hand and varied. Give each of the players a sheet of paper and a pencil and pass round the pillow-case for them all to feel. No one may look inside the pillow-case, all they can do is feel the contents. When everyone has had a good feel, tell them all to write down as many of the objects in the pillow-case as they can. The player with the longest and most accurate list wins the game.

Missing Vowels *

Number: any number   *Age:* 7 upwards   *Time:* 2–3 minutes
(depending on number of words and age of players)   *Adult supervision:* preparation of game and judging answers
(*Equipment:* 1 list of words and 1 pencil per player)

You'll have to prepare this game before the party, and if there are a lot of guests coming delegate it to your children once you have produced a master copy. The game involves replacing vowels in words which have had them removed. Use a children's dictionary to select twenty (possibly more) words and write these out 1 to 20 with dashes in place of the vowels, leaving enough space for the players to write in the missing letters. Then pass the master copy over to your children and ask them to prepare one fair copy for every player. If they are going to compete themselves, make sure they don't look up the answers (better still give them a surprise list on the day!). When completed, fold the papers.

When you come to play the game, give each player a pencil and one of the folded question sheets. When everyone is ready, say 'Go!' and let them open their sheets and start filling in the missing vowels. When the time is up, the player with the most correct answers is the winner. If you plan to give prizes, be prepared for everyone to win; a chocolate button each is fine and if there's only one winner, give a small packet instead of dividing it up.

HOME ENTERTAINMENT

Hand Puppets

Number: any number   *Age:* 6 upwards   *Time:* 10–15 minutes
Adult supervision: demonstrating how to paint puppets
(*Equipment:* non-toxic washable paints in various colours, 1
paintbrush per child)

Hand puppets are the easiest puppets to create. Children can either paint
puppets onto one another's hands and fists, or onto their own.
Whichever they choose, they are sure to have a lot of fun designing and
colouring their chosen puppets.

   It is probably a good idea to give a quick demonstration before they
start. Emphasize the importance of trying to be as clean as possible and
cover the work area with old newspaper or a dust-sheet to catch any
splashes or spills.

   Start painting the puppet by holding your non-painting hand in
front of you, with the fist clenched and the back of the hand in the easiest
position to be painted. Choose the colour for the puppet's face and paint
this onto the back of your hand below the knuckles and above the wrists.
Next comes the hair which is painted over the knuckles and fingers as far
as the first joint. These two colours will give you the basic shape of the
puppet's face. Details like eyes, eyebrows and mouth can be added next,

followed perhaps by a collar and tie, or a scarf to complete the puppet's head. Keep your fist clenched to prevent the face distorting as the paint dries. Then, when you want to create another puppet, simply wash your hands and start again. It is important not to use indelible inks which can be very difficult to remove. Check too that the paints are non-toxic.

Hand puppets painted like this aren't restricted to human faces. Animals can be painted too and if the little finger and index finger are raised above an animal's face, these can be painted to look like horns or ears.

Magic Discs

Number: any number   *Age:* any age   *Time:* 30 seconds per demonstration, allow three minutes for puzzling over it   *Adult supervision:* setting up trick and showing how it works (if no child can demonstrate)   *(Equipment:* a conical-shaped glass, such as a cocktail glass, one light counter or plastic disc, another disc of greater diameter which will fit into the glass higher up.)

Put the glass in full view of the children who should be sitting on the floor. Place the smaller disc in the bottom and the larger one further up, so that both are resting horizontally inside. (Before the trick is shown, make sure that there is adequate clearance between the two to let the larger one revolve without snagging the lower one.)

Now ask the children how it is possible to remove the smaller disc from the glass without touching either of them and without turning the glass upside down. This should cause some puzzling. If anyone has an idea, let them try it out. Unless it is the right one, no one will succeed. When it looks as if all methods have failed, show them how it works. Give a sharp puff on the edge of the upper disc. This will make it tilt upright for a fraction of a second as it spins round. In that time the rush of air into the glass will flip the smaller disc out of the top of the glass and onto the table. If you puff hard enough, the discs may move so fast that the children won't even see them moving. Now let them all have a go.

Lifting the Ice Cube

Number: any number   *Age:* any age   *Time:* 3–5 minutes
Adult supervision: demonstrating the trick   (*Equipment:* a cup
of water, an ice cube, a piece of string, some salt)

How can anyone lift an ice cube from a cup of water with a piece of
string? That's the question put to every audience that watches this trick.
How indeed? They will suggest that you loop the string round the ice
cube and lift it out that way. Let them try this and they will find that the
ice is far too slippery and just slides away whenever they try to lift it.
What's the answer then? A little elementary science as it turns out.

Give the children a chance to see if they can get the ice cube out of
the cup. When it's plain that they can't, show them how to do it. First of
all soak the string, if it isn't thoroughly saturated already. Now lay part
of it on top of the ice cube. Sprinkle salt on both the string and the ice
cube. Leave it for a minute or so and then lift the ice cube triumphantly
from the cup on the end of the string.

How does it work? The salt melts the ice wherever it lands. Then the
lower temperature of the ice freezes the salted area once more. During
this time the string will have become attached to the ice cube and it will
be possible to lift it from the cup.

Have spare ice cubes, cups and pieces of string if you want the
children to experiment for themselves.

Age Telling

Number: any number   *Age:* any age   *Time:* 1–2 minutes per
demonstration   *Adult supervision:* either performing trick or
showing one child how to do it   (*Equipment:* set of six cards
filled with ages as described, possibly paper and pencil for
addition)

This party piece requires preparation beforehand, but once prepared can
be used time and again.

Take six cards and copy the numbers onto each one as indicated by
the chart given below. All you do then is hand the six cards to one of the
players and ask him to tell you the ones on which his age appears. By
adding the first number on each card named you can discover how old
the guest is. Simple, isn't it?

These are the cards you need to prepare:

Card No. 1		Card No. 2		Card No. 3	
1	29	2	30	4	30
3	31	3	31	5	31
5	33	6	34	6	36
7	35	7	35	7	37
9	37	10	38	12	38
11	39	11	39	13	39
13	41	14	42	14	44
15	43	15	43	15	45
17	45	18	46	20	46
19	47	19	47	21	47
21	49	22	50	22	52
23	51	23	51	23	53
25	53	26	54	28	54
27	55	27	55	29	55

Card No. 4		Card No. 5		Card No. 6	
8	28	16	28	32	44
9	29	17	29	33	45
10	30	18	30	34	46
11	31	19	31	35	47
12	40	20	48	36	48
13	41	21	49	37	49
14	42	22	50	38	50
15	43	23	51	39	51
24	44	24	52	40	52
25	45	25	53	41	53
26	46	26	54	42	54
27	47	27	55	43	55

You might like to let your guests copy these cards to try the trick out on their own parents and friends.

Tongue Twisters

Number: any number   *Age:* any age (choose tongue twisters to suit age of players)   *Time:* 3–5 minutes   *Adult supervision:* saying tongue twisters in the first place

Tongue Twisters can be enormous fun either played in a circle with everyone taking it in turns to get their tongue round the twister, or with everyone joining in to chant the twister in unison.

It's probably best to gear your tongue twisters to suit the ages of the players, though you may be surprised by the ease with which some children can manage really difficult ones. Anyhow, here are some classic ones that have provided home entertainment for generations of players:

Bad Blood (repeat ten times very quickly).
Round and round the rugged rocks the ragged rascal ran.
She's so selfish she should sell shellfish, but shellfish shells
    seldom sell.
The rat ran by the river with a lump of raw liver.
Pure food for four pure mules.
The sixth sheik's sixth sheep's sick.
Which wristwatches are Swiss wristwatches.
Double bubble gumbubbles double.
Sister Suzie says she shall shortly sew a sheet.
That bloke's brake-block broke.
Dressed in drip-dry drawers.
The new nuns knew the true nuns knew the new nuns too.
Groovy gravy, baby!
Thin sticks, thick bricks.
Do drop in at the Dewdrop Inn.

And for something more challenging:

Peter Piper picked a peck of pickled peppers. A peck of pickled
peppers Peter Piper picked. If Peter Piper picked a peck of
pickled peppers, where's the peck of pickled peppers Peter
Piper picked?

Disappearing Coin

Number: any number   *Age:* any age   *Time:* 30 seconds per demonstration (let everyone have a go)   *Adult supervision:* demonstrating the trick (only if no child can do it)   *(Equipment:* a bowl of water, a coin, a syringe or small syphoning tube)

Simple conjuring tricks always entertain at parties provided they are quick and work. If you have a professional conjurer coming to your party, obviously it's better to leave any magic to him. But if you want a quiet way of entertaining your guests after tea maybe, a few easy tricks can be great fun. You can also show the children how they work and let them try them out for themselves.

This one involves a simple optical illusion. Place a bowl of water on a table (with a towel underneath in case of accidents). Drop the coin into the bowl and let the water settle. It's a good idea to insert the syringe or syphon tube below the surface at the same time. Now invite one of the children to look into the bowl, lowering his head until the eyes are lined up with the rim of the bowl and the nearside edge of the coin. Tell the child to keep looking in this position while you make the coin disappear. You then gently syphon out some of the water until the coin vanishes. All you have to do to 'replace' it, is to squirt the water just as gently back into the bowl and, hey presto, the coin will appear again!

The trick works thanks to the reflective properties of water. Although the viewer thinks he is looking at the edge of the coin, what is seen is only a reflection. By changing the water-level in the bowl this reflection is moved, and from the original viewpoint it disappears.

Let the children try the trick out on each other, reminding them that it works best if they disturb the water as little as possible.

The Game of Shadows

Number: any number   *Age:* any age   *Time:* 10 minutes   *Adult supervision:* setting up sheet and lamp, and seeing that no one trips over in the dark   *(Equipment:* a white sheet, some means of suspending this as a screen, a lamp, clothes and hats for disguise)

You'll need a black-out for this game, so it's one best played at winter parties. It also requires a certain amount of preparation during the party itself and it's a good idea to occupy the children with another game while everything if being set up. The preparation is well worth the effort and the *Game of Shadows* can be one of the most successful home entertainments.

Hang your white sheet at one end of the room, leaving 2–2.5 metres (6–7½ feet) space behind so that you can position the lamp that will cast the shadows. Tuck the flex well out of harm's way.

The way you use the shadows depends very much on the players. You can either sit one player in front of the screen and parade the others behind it in disguise, seeing how many can be identified by their shadows, or you can divide the players into two teams to do the same thing. It's surprising how easily a child can hide his real identity by holding a finger over a nose or putting on large clothes and hats that hide his shape. Play this game for as long as the children want; they will enjoy experimenting with it.

Shadow Shows

Number: any number   *Age:* any age   *Time:* 5–10 minutes (longer if wanted)   *Adult supervision:* giving a few examples to get the game going   (*Equipment:* a lamp or torch and an area of blank wall)

For one of the simplest forms of home entertainment, *Shadow Shows* offer a huge variety of possibilities and open up great opportunities for players to develop their own skills.

To stage a *Shadow Show* you need only a darkened room, an area of blank wall, and a lamp or torch standing on a table and shining at the wall. From then on it's up to the players to place their hands between the light and the wall, without getting their bodies in the way, making shapes with their hands and forearms to cast life-like shadows on the wall. It's amazing how many different shapes can be created, from birds and rabbits to men wearing hats, and swans gliding over lakes. Practise a few shapes of your own to use as demonstrations and then let the children have a go; at least two can try at any one time, working from opposite sides.

ALLSORTS

Games for Journeys
Games for Holidays
Seaside Games
Seasonal Games
Sickbed Games

GAMES FOR JOURNEYS

Hic, Haec, Hoc *

Number: 2   *Age;* 4 upwards   *Time:* under 15 seconds a round, predetermined number of rounds per game   *Adult supervision:* only to explain rules (if you're driving, certainly no more than that – if that!))

Hic, Haec, Hoc are three Latin words meaning 'this' (they all mean the same), but they also form the name for one of the oldest games of chance played all over the world, which makes it highly suitable for a travelling game. In the past Latin was a common language in many countries so, even though it isn't used today except in certain unusual circumstances, the Latin title is appropriate. The game has an English name, too, *Scissors, Paper, Stone,* which may tell you a lot more about it, but still lacks the style of the Latin!
  The three objects 'Scissors, Paper, Stone' are all indicated by different positions of a player's hand:

Two fingers opened to make a V represent scissors.
An open hand with the fingers closed together represents
   paper.
A clenched fist represents stone.

  To play the game the players hide their playing hands from each other and form one of the three positions as they say together: 'Hic, Haec, Hoc'. As the third word ends they show their playing hands in the position chosen. One of them will be the winner if the hands are in different positions. If they are in the same position, the round is a draw and they try again.
  The winning positions are governed by these simple rules:

Scissors can cut paper – so an open hand loses to fingers in a V.
Paper may wrap stone – so a fist loses to an open hand.
Stone can blunt scissors – so fingers in a V lose to a fist.

  The player who wins a round wins a point, and after the set number of rounds, say twenty, the player with the most points wins the game.

Mora *

Number: 2   *Age:* 5 upwards   *Time:* less than 15 seconds a
round, games of 10–15 rounds   *Adult supervision:* only to
explain rules and stop the noise from getting too loud

Mora is another very old game, rather like *Hic, Haec, Hoc*, in which
players show their hands at the same time and try to predict what will be
shown.

In this case the players have to guess how many fingers will be
shown altogether (in *Mora* the thumbs are also counted as fingers). The
players begin a round with one hand clenched on their chests. At an
agreed signal they both throw open their hands showing a certain
number of fingers, or show a clenched fist which represents nought. At
the same time each player calls a number, guessing the total of fingers
shown. If one player calls 'Mora!' it means he is banking on ten fingers
being shown. The player who makes the correct guess wins the round
and a point. If both guess correctly the round is a draw. And if neither
guesses correctly the round is void.

The player with the most points after an agreed number of rounds
wins the game.

Shoot *

Number: 2   *Age:* 5 upwards   *Time:* less than 15 seconds a
round, games run to 10–15 rounds   *Adult supervision:* only to
explain rules and keep control if the game becomes too rowdy

Shoot shares many similarities with *Mora*, the principal difference being
that instead of guessing how many fingers will be shown, the players try
to guess whether the total will be odd or even. The other major difference
is that both hands may be used, offering a range of numbers from 1 to 20.

As they throw open their hands the players shout 'Odds!' or
'Evens!', and they count the fingers to see who wins as in *Mora*. (In *Shoot*
the closed fist of nought counts as an even number.)

The winner is the player with the most points after the agreed
number of rounds.

Number-Plate Numbers *

Number: any number   *Age:* 4 upwards   *Time:* 5–10 minutes
Adult supervision: only to explain rules and maybe help by
joining in

The aim of this game is to count from 1 to 20, and to do so by spotting all twenty figures on the number-plates of passing cars. The first player to spot a number gets it, so keep a sharp look-out.

Only one number can be obtained from each number-plate, so a car with the number CDD 132 will give you 1 or 13 or 2 or 3, but not all four of them! When you get into double figures the numbers on the number-plate must be in the right order; in the example above you could have 13, but *not* 12.

The first player to get to 20 wins the game.

Alphabetical Sentences *

Number: any number   *Age:* 6 upwards   *Time:* 10 minutes
Adult supervision: only to explain rules and judge answers
(*Equipment:* paper and pencil per player)

This is a game best played somewhere that is comfortable and easy to write in, and is therefore more suited for a journey by train, aeroplane or ship.

Each player is given a pencil and paper and ten minutes in which to compose the longest alphabetical sentence he or she can think of, that is a sentence which has words starting with letters in alphabetical order. The first word must start with A, the second with B, the third with C, the fourth with D, and so on. Each word scores 1 point. The player with the highest score wins.

So a player who managed this sentence in ten minutes would get 21 points: Angry Baron Calls Deadly Enemy For Grim Holiday In Jolly Knight's Lovely Manor Near Old Perfectly Quiet Rural Spot Towards Upminster – mind you that's pretty good going, most players do well to get into double figures. See how you get on.

Geography *

Number: any number   *Age:* 7 upwards   *Time:* 2–3 minutes
Adult supervision: only to judge answers   (*Equipment:* paper
and pencil for each player)

This is a game that is probably best played on a train or aeroplane, rather than a car. However, if the players can manage to write reasonably well in a car, by all means take it with you on the road.

The beauty of this game is that it can be made as easy or as difficult as the skill of the players demands. On the easiest level the players have to find the names of nine places, each of which begins with one of the letters that spell GEOGRAPHY. So a simple answer to this might be:

> Guernsey
> Egypt
> Oman
> Gibraltar
> Rome
> Athens
> Portugal
> Hungary
> Yugoslavia

Here the answer includes the names of countries, cities and one island. To make the game more challenging it could be limited to cities. On the other hand you might prefer to play the game in each of the continents.

You can play the game in any way you choose, providing that all the players have an even chance. They just write GEOGRAPHY down the left side of the sheet of paper and fill in the words on the word 'Go!'. The first player to complete a correct list wins the game.

Number-Plate Messages *

Number: any number   *Age:* 6 upwards   *Time:* 5–10 minutes
Adult supervision: only to explain rules and point out suitable
number-plates

In this game the driver gives each player in turn the letters of a different number-plate and the players have to turn these into special messages.

Any player who can't think of a message must drop out, and the last player left giving messages wins the game.

Each word of the message must begin with one of the letters from the number-plate, used in the same order. For example, the letters FCD might produce messages like:

> Free Canned Doughnuts
> Four Course Dinner
> Freshly Dug Cabbages
> Food Canteen Door

and so on.

Sir Tommy

Number: 1   *Age:* 8 upwards   *Time:* 10 minutes or more
Adult supervision: none (once the game has been explained)
(*Equipment:* a pack of cards)

Travelling on a long journey can be a tiring business, and at times it's good to know a quiet game which a child can play on his own. *Sir Tommy* suits this aim well, because it's one of the oldest-known forms of patience and can keep children absorbed for hours.

The objective is to build up four ascending sequences from ace to king, regardless of suit and colour. Cards are dealt out from the pack one at a time on to any of four face-up waste piles. The aces when they turn up are used to form four foundations next to the waste piles.

The foundations may be built on, placing any 2 on any ace, any 3 on any 2, and so on. The top card of any waste pile may be played on to a foundation in this way, but cards may not be transferred from one waste pile to another.

The pack is dealt out only once – there is no second chance. There is a small amount of skill involved in the decision as to which waste pile a card from the pack is dealt, but it is simply a matter of avoiding the necessity of covering a low-ranking card with a high one.

Spoof *

Number: 2 or more   *Age:* 5 upwards   *Time:* 30 seconds a round,
10–15 rounds per game   *Adult supervision:* only to explain
rules, provide counters and keep control (if necessary)
(*Equipment:* three counters, or coins, per player)

Spoof is a game of bluff and guesswork, appealing to players of all ages,
in which the players try to guess the total number of counters, or coins,
they are each hiding in their clenched fists.

A round starts with all the players hiding some or none of their
counters in one fist. The fists are outstretched and one by one the players
call out a total they think might be hidden in all the fists. The calls move
to the left, and after the last player has called, the fists are opened and the
total number of counters is counted. The player who either guessed the
correct total, or who came nearest to guessing it, wins the round. After
the agreed number of rounds has been played, the winner is the player
with the most points.

Mile's End *

Number: any number   *Age:* 4 upwards   *Time:* 1–2 minutes
depending on car's speed   *Adult supervision:* to give starting
signal and decide winner   (*Equipment:* car mileometer)

The object of this game is for the players to guess distances as accurately
as possible. The driver will tell the players to 'Get ready!' and 'Start'.
They then sit back and wait until they think they have travelled exactly
one mile, at which point they must shout 'Now!'.

This game is best played with eyes closed, or if the players promise
not to cheat by looking at the speedometer, they can play with their eyes
open (which will help them spot markers on the roadside).

The player with the most accurate guess wins the game.

Word Watching *

Number: any number   *Age:* 6 upwards   *Time:* 5–10 minutes
Adult supervision: only to explain rules and possibly keep
score   (*Equipment:* paper and pencil per player)

This is another game to be played with the letters of car number-plates.
This time players have to keep their eyes open for complete words on the
number-plates. These will be three-letter words, for example:

DAD	BAR
CAT	BEE
BUG	EAT
TOE	OAT

Score one point for each word. However, after noting down the
words, keep an eye open for others that might be added onto them to
form six-letter words. Any one of these earns five bonus points! Some
possible combinations are:

CAR	PET
TEA	POT
FOR	GET
CAT	KIN

The player who has the highest score after a set period of time wins
the game.

Build-Up *

Number: any number   *Age:* 8 upwards   *Time:* 10–15 minutes
Adult supervision: only to explain rules and check answers
(*Equipment:* paper and pencil per player)

In this game the players are given a word and have to see how many new
words they can build up from it, using the original word to start with
each time. Decide on the time limit before play begins and before the
word is given. Depending on the age of the players, you may wish to
shorten the time span to prevent the game from dragging on for too long.
Suppose the word given was MAN, the players might be able to produce
words like:

MANAGE
MANGLE
MANGER
MANURE
MANHOLE
MANHANDLE
MANLY
MANSION
MANOR
MANY

Other suitable starter words are: CAT, AIR, DON, EAR, FOR, HEAD, TIN and WATER.

Observation *

Number: any number   *Age:* 7 upwards   *Time:* 10 minutes or longer   *Adult supervision:* only to suggest topics and keep track of the score (if necessary)   (*Equipment:* paper and pencil)

This is a game for those who like keeping their eyes open on a journey by car or train.

Before the game starts the players agree on a list of things they might see and award each a certain number of points. Very common objects and sights only score low points, but a glimpse of something unusual might score a player ten points. Once the list is agreed the players start scanning their route to pinpoint objects on the list and start building their scores. After a set time limit the player with the highest score wins. Only one player can score off each sighting, so the first player to call out 'Look, there's *Concorde*' (or whatever it may be) wins the points.

A typical list might include objects like:

A man pasting posters	5 points
A woman pushing a pram	2 points
A Rolls-Royce	7 points
A breakdown truck	2 points
A police car	1 point

Try to make the list varied and don't be frightened of including some unlikely objects – you'd be surprised how frequently the unexpected can turn up.

A to Z *

Number: any number   *Age:* 6 upwards   *Time:* 5–10 minutes
Adult supervision: only to explain rules and point out possible
letters if the players get stuck   (*Equipment:* paper and pencil
to record letters)

There are few things more annoying when you are on a long journey than
to be snarled up in thick traffic as you drive through a town or city. One
of the ways of making the best of this annoying predicament is to
propose a game of *A to Z*, for which travelling slowly through a built-up
area is a positive advantage.

The players have to collect the letters of the alphabet as they pass
words and letters on signs, in shop window displays, on posters or on
other cars. Each player keeps his eyes open on the look-out for the next
letter in the alphabet, and whichever player sees it first scores one point.
By the time the game has reached Z, the player with the highest score is
the winner.

The letters can come from any source seen from the car, but each
source can only provide one letter. In the case of the A–Z Cleaners, for
example, only one of those letters can be used, and it would have to be in
the right alphabetical sequence – in other words, at the beginning or
end of the game.

Fish *

Number: any number   *Age:* 6 upwards   *Time:* 3–5 minutes
Adult supervision: only to explain rules and possibly play a
hand   (*Equipment:* a pack of playing cards)

All you need to play this game (apart from the playing cards) is a flat
surface. A table on board a train is ideal, but you may be able to rig up a
flat surface in the back of the car, or on the seat between the players.

The game begins with each player being dealt five cards. The
remainder are placed face down on the table. The first player to play is
the one to the left of the dealer. He asks one of the others for a particular
card, after studying the cards in his hand. The object of the game is to
form sets of four cards (four aces, four 2s, four kings, four 5s etc.) and to
get rid of all one's cards by doing this. So if a player has one or more of a
particular set, he can ask any other player for another to match it. If the
player has the card, he hands it over. If the card isn't in that player's hand

then the player says 'Fish!', and the one who asked for it must fish the top card from the reserve pile. The player who said 'Fish!' is the next to play.

When a player has collected a set of four cards of the same value these are put down on the table. The first player to get rid of all his cards wins.

Colour Contest *

Number: any number   *Age:* 4 upwards   *Time:* 15 minutes, or 15 miles, is a good time, but longer or shorter periods can be used
Adult supervision: giving players colours to look out for

In this simple game the driver awards each player a colour. It might be red. It might be blue. It might be green. But it's unlikely to be purple or pink, because the colours must all be those used fairly frequently for cars, and purple and pink cars don't crop up that often.

Once the players have been given their colours and they know the time limit for the game, they try to spot as many cars of their colour as they can. The driver can keep a mental note of these, too, if there is no other adult passenger to do this.

At the end of the time limit the player with the most cars in his or her colour is the winner and may choose the next game to be played.

GAMES FOR HOLIDAYS

Islands *

Number: any number   *Age:* 5 upwards   *Time:* 5 minutes
Adult supervision: only to prevent rough play   (*Equipment:* means to mark a circle, ties for ankles)

If you want a game that's going to burn up surplus holiday energy, *Islands* is ideal for a group of children about the same age. It's simple too, though it should only be played on soft ground like grass or on a beach, not on concrete.

Just mark a circle about 3 metres (10 feet) across with chalk, or using a stick in sand or earth, tie each player's ankles together and stand them at intervals around the circle, about 5 metres (16 feet) away from it. On the word 'Go!' they must fold their arms and start hopping towards the Island (circle). Once there, they have to try and prevent anyone else from landing, but must keep their arms folded all the time.

If the children are about the same size, no one is likely to get hurt. Everyone is sure to have great fun defending the island without being thrown off at the same time.

Queenie

Number: any number (the more the merrier)   *Age:* 6 upwards
Time: 10 minutes   *Adult supervision:* only to explain rules
(*Equipment:* a ball)

One of the players is chosen to start the game as Queenie, and she stands at the end of the playing area (the larger the better, and definitely out of doors) with her back to the other players. On the word 'Go!' she throws the ball over her shoulder and counts to five. The other players all scramble for the ball. When Queenie reaches five she shouts 'Stop!' and the others must stand stock still with their hands behind their backs. Queenie then turns round and must try to guess who has the ball. If she guesses correctly, the player with the ball becomes Queenie for the next round. If her guess is wrong, she remains Queenie, collects the ball, turns her back on the others and throws it over her shoulder once again.

Corko *

Number: any number   *Age:* 6 upwards   *Time:* 5–10 minutes
Adult supervision: only to explain rules and demonstrate
flicking technique   (*Equipment:* at least three corks and a
good-sized bucket)

Corko is a simple 'shooting' game which can be played almost any-where. Start by marking a 'flicking' line from which the players must flick corks at a bucket, placed about 3 metres (10 feet) away. The players stand on the line and take it in turns to try and flick the corks into the bucket. Flicking is done by using the thumb and forefinger of one hand.

Players score one point for one cork in the bucket, five for two corks and ten if all three corks land in it.

The first player to score fifty wins.

The Boiler Burst!

Number: any number   *Age:* 7 upwards   *Time:* 2–3 minutes
Adult supervision: none except to judge who last crosses the line, where necessary

This is a silly game which has been popular with children for generations. It's easy to play, fun to listen to and has an unexpected climax which all the players enjoy.

Play begins with one of the group starting to tell a story, with the others clustered round to listen. The story can be as short or as drawn-out as the player wants, but it must always end with the totally unexpected announcement 'And then the boiler burst!'

The moment the players hear this, they all dash for a pre-arranged line and the last one over must tell the story in the next round.

Pavement Bullboard *

Number: any number   *Age:* 7 upwards   *Time:* 5 minutes per round   *Adult supervision:* possibly to mark out playing area
(*Equipment:* something to mark out playing area and a button or counter for the players to throw)

This game can be played on any level surface. Its name comes from its original setting – a street pavement – but it can be played as well on a gravel or earth surface.

5	6
4	7
3	8
2	9
1	10

Start by marking out a simple grid like the one on the previous page, and number the squares from 1 to 10. The players then take it in turns to throw the button or counter into the squares numbered from 1 to 10 one after the other. Players who miss squares 3 or 9 miss a turn and must start right back at number 1. Players who miss other numbers lose a turn, but are allowed to continue on their way from the square they missed once they have landed the button or counter in it. The first one to reach square 10 wins the game.

Crossing Out Letters *

Number: any number   *Age:* 7 upwards   *Time:* 5–10 minutes
Adult supervision: only to make sure that the papers used aren't 'Today's'!

Killing time during school holidays can often be a problem, and if the weather has turned against playing outside when a group of friends are together, you might find this an ideal way of entertaining them.

The game can be played in two ways, both involving old newspapers, so check before play starts that the papers are due to be thrown away, because after the game they won't be of much use.

The players can either be given the same page from the same edition of the newspaper, or they can be given different sheets. In both cases they must cross out specific words or letters. If they all have the same sheet, the first player to cross out the relevant words or letters wins. If the sheets are different, the players play against the clock. After a set time limit, the one with the greatest number of words or letters crossed out wins the game.

You might tell them to cross out every 'B' on their page, or every 'T' or 'R'. On the other hand, a more difficult version makes the players cross out specific words – 'and' or 'but' or 'in', for example.

Whichever way you play, the game is fun and challenging.

Slap Jack

Number: any number (the larger the better)   *Age:* 6 upwards
Time: 10 minutes or more   *Adult supervision:* only to explain
rules

The game begins with all the players standing in a circle, facing inwards,
their hands behind their backs. One player is chosen as 'He', and moves
out of the circle, running round the back of it, slapping the hands of one
of the players as he passes. 'He' carries on running round the circle and
the players whose hands have been slapped immediately leaves his
place and runs round the circle in the opposite direction as fast as he can,
in an attempt to beat 'He' to the space in the circle.

If the player whose hands were slapped succeeds in returning to the
space before 'He', 'He' must remain as 'He' for the next round. But if 'He'
beats the player to the space, they change places and the new 'He' must
try to slap another player's hands and race him to the space in the next
round.

Snow Snake *

Number: 4 or more   *Age:* 7 upwards   *Time:* 5 minutes
Adult supervision: preparing sticks and judging rounds
(if necessary)   (*Equipment:* 3–5 sticks per player)

Snow Snake is a winter game developed by North American Indians. It
can be played on smooth firm unbroken snow and is really a very simple
game, although a certain amount of judgment is very useful in choosing
when to use high-scoring sticks.

The players stand on a throwing line with their sticks in hand.
These should be small sticks, whittled smooth so that they will slide
over the snow. One stick will have one notch cut in it, another two
notches, a third three notches, a fourth four and the fifth five notches
(assuming each player has five sticks). Players take turns to throw their
sticks, one per round. The stick that travels furthest in each round wins,
and the player scores points according to the number of notches on the
sticks. This is where the skill comes in. Players need not throw their
sticks in the order of the notches. They may be thrown in any order, with
players choosing when to use their high-scoring sticks and when to
throw the low-scoring ones. The player with the highest score after the
last round has been played is the winner.

Triangular Tug of War *

Number: 3   *Age:* 7 upwards   *Time:* 1–3 minutes   *Adult supervision:* only to provide equipment and tie rope securely (*Equipment:* length of strong rope about 8 metres (26 feet) long and 3 objects)

Here is an energetic open-air game which can be enjoyed by just three players. The rope is safely knotted to form a loop and is handed to the players who stand in a triangle, each one taking the rope with one hand. About 1 metre (3 feet) behind each player is placed an object like a ball, a hat, a coat, a pullover or a stone. The aim of the game is for the players to tug the rope far enough to allow them to pick up the objects behind them, but of course with each player pulling in a different direction, this can be quite a struggle. The first player to succeed in picking up his object is the winner.

Newspaper Quiz *

Number: 2–4   *Age:* 8 upwards   *Time:* 5–10 minutes   *Adult supervision:* acting as question-master   (*Equipment:* 2 copies of the same newspaper)

This is a game for two small teams and a question-master. Both teams are given copies of the same newspaper and are allowed five minutes to study them. When they have had a chance to look through them, the question-master asks a series of questions on different topics – the answers to all of which can be found in the papers. The first team to come up with the correct answer wins a point, and the team with the highest score after twenty questions wins the game.

Squat Tag

Number: any number   *Age:* 6 upwards   *Time:* 2–3 minutes   *Adult supervision:* only to see that no player squats more times than allowed (if necessary)

This is an appealing variation on the common game of *Tag* in which players may avoid being caught by 'It' by squatting. 'It' decides how many squats to allow the others before the game begins. The wise players save their squats until the last minute when 'It' is just about to tag them. Those who use up their squats too quickly, find that they have to spend the rest of the game running as fast as they can. The first player tagged becomes 'It'.

Touch Tag

Number: any number   *Age:* 7 upwards   *Time:* 3–5 minutes
Adult supervision: only to ensure rules are followed

In this popular version of *Tag* the player tagged must place a hand on that part of his body and hold it there while running round to try and tag another player. Players tagged by touches on the back have to hold a hand behind their back. Those tagged on an arm must chase their prey with their hand on their arm, and any players unlucky enough to be tagged on a foot have to hop around in the hope of tagging someone else!

Eh, Bee, Sea *

Number: 2 or more   *Age:* 8 upwards   *Time:* 10 minutes   *Adult supervision:* only to check answers   (*Equipment:* paper and pencil for each player)

This is an alphabet game with a difference. Each player is given a paper and pencil and has ten minutes in which to write down words (including proper names) that sound like letters of the alphabet – words like:

Eh?	A
Bee	B
Sea/See	C

After ten minutes the player with the longest list wins.

To make the game a little more difficult, you can also allow words that sound like two or more letters of the alphabet. For example:

Eyes	I's	Envy	NV
Empty	MT	Ivy	IV
Ewes	U's	Eighty	AT
Jail	JL	Enemy	NME
City	CT	Icy	IC

and so on.

In either case the player with the longest list wins.

SEASIDE GAMES

Beach Golf *

Number: any number *Age:* 7 upwards *Time:* 15 minutes or more *Adult supervision:* only to see that the 'course' doesn't take up too much of the beach! (*Equipment:* used ice-cream cartons, a club and ball)

If you find several empty, round ice-cream cartons, they can become part of a small golf-course on the beach, before finally making their way to the rubbish bin. The cartons can be sunk into the sand at intervals to act as holes. There is no need for the course to cover a large area, especially if doing this would be obviously anti-social. Nine holes would be fine, and children can have great fun constructing bunkers and other obstacles leading to the holes. They can also mark the holes with paper flags, if they want. For a club you can use almost anything from the genuine article to a piece of driftwood, and since you won't be encouraging them to hit the ball for hundreds of yards, a small soft ball that will drop into an ice-cream carton is probably the best bet.

You could find that the creation of the course takes up far longer than the game itself and may occupy children happily all day long until the tide flows in and washes it all way. (Before you leave the beach, however, make sure the ice-cream cartons are thrown away – in a rubbish bin, of course!)

Pin Weed *

Number: 2 or more *Age:* 7 upwards *Time:* 5 minutes
Adult supervision: only to explain rules and possibly set up 'equipment' (*Equipment:* 3 pieces of driftwood about a metre (3 feet) long and 3 large strong strands of seaweed)

At the start of this game you will have to set up the playing area with the three pieces of wood planted in the sand at one end. Stick them one in front of the other, about 2 metres (6½ feet) apart, with about half of each one above the surface. The players line up at the throwing line about 5 metres (16 feet) in front of these 'pins'.

Each player is given the three strands of seaweed in turn and can make several attempts to throw them so that they wrap themselves around one of the pins. Five points are scored for weed wrapped round the first pin, ten if it wraps round the second, and fifteen if it wraps round the third. A throw counts as long as some part of the weed is touching one of the pins, so it's possible to score as much as forty-five if you are very lucky.

At the end of a pre-arranged number of rounds the player with the highest score is the winner.

Hopscotch *

Number: any number *Age:* 6 upwards *Time:* 10 minutes
Adult supervision: possibly to mark out playing area
(*Equipment:* marker of some description and a pebble)

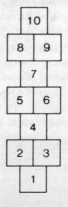

Starting line ————

Although *Hopscotch* was first played on pavements or playgrounds, it's ideally suited for playing on the beach where the playing area can be drawn easily in the sand (the best sand is the wet, firm sand near the shoreline).

You'll need to mark out a playing area as shown above before you start to play. Each of the squares in the ten-square plan is about 50 cms (18 inches) wide and the design should look like the illustration.

Once the playing area is ready, the players line up on the starting line and take it in turns to throw a pebble into one of the ten squares. If the pebble falls outside the playing area, or lands on one of the lines, the thrower loses his turn. If the pebble does land in one of the squares, the player must go to that square, hopping through every single square and landing with both feet on the double squares. Once in the right square, the player picks up the pebble and marks his initials in one corner. Touching any of the lines during the hopping also loses a turn.

The first player to write his initials in all ten squares wins.

Water Relay *

Number: any large even number   *Age:* 5 upwards   *Time:* 3–5 minutes   *Adult supervision:* only to explain rules and probably provide materials   (*Equipment:* 2 tins of plastic containers filled with water, a reservoir of water)

The beach is a perfect place to play this relay game, which under other conditions might result in piles of wet clothing. The players divide into two equal teams and sit one behind the other in two rows. The player at the head of each row is given a container filled to the brim with water. On the word 'Go!' the tins are passed backwards down the line, over the players' heads to the players at the end of each line. They then run with the container to refill it if water has been spilt before sitting at the head of their respective lines and passing the container back down the line for the next round. When the original player at the head of the line returns to the front the passing stops and the first team to achieve this wins.

The containers must be kept full of water throughout the game, and if the sea is near enough it makes sense to fill them from that.

Middle Man *

Number: any large number   *Age:* 6 upwards   *Time:* 5–10 minutes   *Adult supervision:* only to explain rules and possibly act as judge   (*Equipment:* 1 ball)

The players form a circle with one of them standing in the middle with the ball. The game begins with the player in the middle throwing the ball to one of those in the circle and then immediately changing places with another player in the circle. The player whose place has been taken must try to catch the ball in the middle of the circle, before it is thrown across to the other side. Any player who fails to do this leaves the circle, and the last successful one to run from the circle and catch the ball before it crosses to the other side starts in the middle in the next round.

French Cricket

Number: any number   *Age:* 6 upwards   *Time:* 10–15 minutes *Adult supervision:* only to explain rules and probably join in   (*Equipment:* small cricket bat or old tennis racquet, and tennis ball)

This popular beach game is one that can be enjoyed by all the family. One player is given the bat at the start of the game and has to defend his legs from the ball thrown by the others who are ranged round on all sides. The player with the bat must keep his feet still until he has hit the ball. However, he can twist round and hold the bat at the back of his legs, or change from one side to the other as often as necessary, providing the feet don't move.

The other players aim to get the batsman out by throwing the ball to hit his legs below the knees. The ball can be passed quickly from player to player to confuse the batsman, but the player who succeeds in hitting the legs is given the bat next. The batsman can also be caught out, and an entertaining variation is to allow fielders to catch the batsman out 'one-hand-one-bounce', which means that if the ball bounces once but is caught single-handed, the batsman and the catcher must swap places.

French Cricket is a fast-moving, entertaining game in which the players with the bat are constantly changing, giving everyone a fair chance to have a go.

Twigs *

Number: 2   *Age:* 7 upwards   *Time:* 5–10 minutes   *Adult supervision:* only to explain rules and see they are followed
(*Equipment:* a handful of small twigs or sticks)

Twigs is a perfect game to be played on the beach immediately after lunch. It is quiet and absorbing, and will give children time to digest their food before they can go swimming again.

At the start of the game two of the twigs are stuck in the sand about 10 centimetres (4 inches) apart. Each player is then given an equal number of the remaining twigs with which to play and the players take it in turns to move.

The first begins by drawing a line in the sand between the two twigs. He then sticks one of his twigs in the sand half way along the line just drawn. The other player must draw a line joining any two of the three twigs now in the sand and stick one of his twigs half way along that line. Play continues like this with the players taking it in turns to join up any two of the twigs in the ground and place another in the middle of the line just drawn. However, the game has more to it than this. *No line may be drawn across another line* and *when a twig has three lines radiating from it, that twig must be removed.*

The first player unable to draw a line because of crossing another loses.

King Canute's Game *

Number: any number   *Age:* 5 upwards   *Time:* half an hour (but you don't 'play' for that long)   *Adult supervision:* judging
(*Equipment:* one stick per player)

Poor King Canute, who got his feet wet teaching his fawning courtiers that he didn't in fact control the waves, has given his name to this simple yet challenging beach game.

Each of the players is given a short stick which acts as a marker. They all study the sea for a few minutes trying to decide how far up the beach the tide will have risen in half an hour. (Make sure you check that the tide *is* rising when you play this game!) Once each player has decided, he plants the marker stick in the sand. When the half-hour is up the sticks are examined and the one nearest the tide level wins.

Beach Olympics *

Number: any number   *Age:* 6 upwards   *Time:* up to half an hour   *Adult supervision:* selecting events according to the beach and judging   (*Equipment:* beach balls, and ties for ankles)

If you have a large group of children with masses of energy on the beach, and if the beach is large enough to let them run around a fairly large area without being a nuisance, you might enjoy organizing some simple *Beach Olympics*. You'll need a track of some sort, marked by a starting line and a finishing post, as well as an umpire, which is most likely to be you. The events are all racing games since throwing anything but light-weight balls around the beach can be dangerous. You will probably think up races of your own, but here are some ideas you might like to try:

1. Hopping Race, first using right feet only for half the course, then changing to left foot.
2. Three-Legged Race, in which players compete in pairs with their ankles tied together.
3. Head-Over-Heels Race, in which players roll down the course in this way. (Check for stones before they do this.)
4. Water Race, with players carrying water and being disqualified for spilling any.
5. Triple Jump Race, in which players hop, skip and jump down the course in that order, repeating it until they cross the finishing line.
6. Piggy-Back Race.
7. Wheelbarrow Race, with players competing in pairs, one as the wheelbarrow walking on his hands while the other holds his legs.
8. Ball-Throwing Race, with players in pairs throwing a ball between them as they race along the track.
9. Backward Race, with players racing backwards down the track.
10. Four-Legged Race, which is just like the three-legged one, except that three players not two take part in each team.

Three Against One *

Number: 4   *Age:* 6 upwards   *Time:* 5–10 minutes
Adult supervision: only to explain rules

In this energetic beach game, suitable for getting children warm again
after swimming, three of the players join hands to form a ring and the
fourth tries to tag a named player by running round the outside of the
ring. The other three run round too, still holding hands and trying to
prevent the one on the outside tagging his prey.

When a player has been tagged, he swaps places with the tagger,
though it's as well to give everyone a chance on the outside to make it
fair.

Skimmers *

Number: any number   *Age:* 7 upwards   *Time:* 5–10 minutes
Adult supervision: making sure that stones are thrown well
away from swimmers   (*Equipment:* 20 flat stones per player)

To play skimmers you will need a stretch of flat sea free from any
swimmers. (Throwing stones into the sea where people are bathing is, of
course, very dangerous.) Each player will need twenty flat stones to skim
across the surface of the water. Let the players choose their own stones,
though show them the sort they should be looking for. These are smooth
flat round stones that fit comfortably between the forefinger and thumb
of the throwing hand.

The aim of the game is to throw the stones close to the surface of the
water, and with sufficient spin, so that they skim across the surface
bouncing up and down. At first, children may find that they can't get
more than one bounce from a stone before it sinks to the bottom, but after
a little practice they will get the knack of aiming low and sending the
stone on a level even flight.

Players who make the stone bounce once score one point. Two
bounces score three points, three bounces score ten points, four bounces
score twenty and five score fifty (six and above score fifty as well). Five
points are lost whenever a stone fails to bounce at all. The first player to
score 200 wins.

The Shebble Game *

Number: 2   *Age:* 7 upwards   *Time:* 2–3 minutes   *Adult supervision:* only to explain rules   (*Equipment:* 12 shells, pebbles, coins or bottle tops)

This beach game gets is name because it can be played with pebbles or shells (or with coins or bottle tops if these are easier to find).

All you need do is arrange the twelve pieces in a circle so that the pebbles, shells, or whatever, are touching. The aim of the game is to be the last player to remove the last object or pair of objects from the circle. The players take it in turns to remove one or two objects at a time, but they can only take two shells or pebbles in one go if they are touching at the time.

The player who removes the last object or objects wins the game.

Catch and Pull *

Number: any equal number   *Age:* 7 upwards   *Time:* 5 minutes *Adult supervision:* only to make sure the game doesn't get too rough   (*Equipment;* a marker (a pebble would do))

This is a beach game for energetic players. A line is marked in the sand, a good thick line which can be seen easily even after it has been trodden on. The players divide into two equal teams and stand on either side of the line. On the word 'Go!' players in both teams attempt to pull players of the other team over the line.

Players may help those on their own side from being pulled over, but once a player has been completely pulled over the line he joins the other side. Arms and legs may be pulled but pulling hair must not be allowed, nor should any rough bullying.

The team with the most players at the end of the allotted time wins.

Squirts *

Number: any number   *Age:* 5 upwards   *Time:* five minutes
Adult supervision: only to explain rules and make sure there is
no cheating   (*Equipment:* one empty plastic detergent bottle per
player and one large bucket, full of water)

For reasons which will become obvious this game must be played in
swimsuits! Each player is armed with a detergent bottle, and a circle is
drawn in the sand inside which the bucket of water is placed. The game
starts with all the players standing outside the circle. On the word 'Go!'
they rush to the bucket of water and fill their bottles by squeezing them
and then releasing the sides as they hold them under the water. Once the
squirters are filled, the players must leave the circle and start squirting
each other on the back, while trying to avoid being squirted themselves.
Once a squirter is empty its owner may run into the circle again to refill
it. The circle is a safe area inside which players may not be squirted. The
player who has the driest back after five minutes squirting wins.

SEASONAL GAMES

Romeo and Juliet (St Valentine's Day)

Number: any number   *Age:* 6 upwards   *Time:* 2–3 minutes
Adult supervision: only to see that the blindfolds are correctly
fitted and that neither player falls over   (*Equipment:* two
blindfolds)

Just in case a children's party happens to fall on or near 14 February, you
may like to include a topical game in the selection of entertainments
offered. In which case this version of *Blindman's Buff* is very suitable.
    Two players, a boy and a girl, are blindfolded and stand in the centre
of a circle formed by the others holding hands. Romeo tries to find Juliet
by calling her name and making his way towards her following her
voice. Juliet must answer but she can alter her voice and move away from
her original position as soon as she has given her reply. The players in
the circle have great fun watching the antics of the pair, who will often
pass very close to each other without actually touching. When Romeo
catches Juliet, another couple take their place.

Heart Throbs (St Valentine's Day)

Number: any number   *Age:* 10 upwards   *Time:* 2 minutes
Adult supervision: only to prevent the game from going too far!

This game is popular in North America at parties held around St Valentine's Day. It is only suitable for older children who may start to be showing more than a passing interest in the opposite sex. It's a harmless game which may help the players to stop taking themselves too seriously.

Choose a boy and girl who are known to have an interest in each other and seat them opposite each other. They take each other's wrists and feel the pulse rate, counting it aloud and looking fixedly into each other's eyes for two minutes. Any smiles, giggles, looks aside or belly laughs brings their turn to an end, and another couple sit down and have a go. If they succeed in keeping quite controlled for two minutes just looking into each other's eyes, you'll know it's as well to keep an eye on them for the rest of the party.

While the Valentine couple are holding wrists and counting aloud, the rest of the players can laugh and talk as much as they like to see how easily they can distract the couple.

Hole in the Sheet (April Fool's Day)

Number: any number   *Age:* 6 upwards   *Time:* 3–5 minutes
Adult supervision: only to make sure the sheet used is one that can have holes cut in it   (*Equipment:* sheet with two holes cut in it, one for the nose, one for a knee-cap)

This is an April Fool's Day game in which there are no winners or losers, but everyone can have great fun. Start by hanging the sheet in a doorway with the small hole at about nose height and the larger hole at knee-height. Half the players must be on one side of the sheet, half on the other side. Both sides take it in turns to choose a player who pushes his nose and a knee-cap through the holes, while the other side guess to whom they belong. The game ends when everyone has had a turn displaying their noses and knees.

Egg Guessing (Easter)

Number: any number   *Age:* 7 upwards   *Time:* 3–5 minutes
Adult supervision: counting number of sweets in egg before
handing it round   (*Equipment:* cardboard Easter egg and supply
of small sweets)

For this popular Easter game, which serves well as an ice-breaker, you
will need a cardboard Easter egg and a collection of small sweets,
carefully counted before they are placed inside the egg.

This is then passed round the group of players sitting on the ground.
They may feel the weight of the egg and may shake it gently, and all must
try and guess how many sweets are inside. The one who comes nearest to
the total wins the sweets, though it's worth hanging on to the egg itself
for future years.

Easter Bunnies and Chicks *

Number: any number   *Age:* 5 upwards   *Time:* 5 minutes
Adult supervision: preparing a course that will be safe for all
players   (*Equipment:* ties for ankles)

If the weather is fine for your Easter party this might be the first chance in
the year to sit outside and enjoy the garden, and naturally your guests
will want to play something appropriate while you relax over a well-
earned cup of tea. *Easter Bunnies and Chicks* is a racing game which
should tire even the most determined athlete in the group.

The game begins with half the players becoming bunnies and the
other half becoming chicks. They line up on the starting line with
bunnies having their ankles tied together and chicks standing on one
leg. On the word 'Go!' they race down the course in this way with the
bunnies hopping along with their feet together and the chicks doing as
best as they can on one leg. The winner is the first across the line. At the
far end the bunnies become chicks and vice versa, and they race back
again.

Easter Egg Relay *

Number: any even number   *Age:* 6 upwards   *Time:* 3–5
minutes   *Adult supervision:* judging   (*Equipment:* 2 cardboard
egg halves, 2 cereal bowls, 2 salt spoons, and a small sugared egg
or candy for each player)

The players are divided into equal teams and stand one behind the other
in two lines. Immediately in front of each team is a cereal bowl and some
distance away are the two cardboard egg halves, one for each team, filled
with sugared eggs or candies. The first player in each team is given a
small salt spoon, and on the word 'Go!' he runs to the cardboard egg and
lifts out one of the sweets with the salt spoon. The players race back to
their own teams, place the sweet in the cereal bowl, give the salt spoon to
the next player and go to the back of the line.

The teams race like this until all the sweets have been safely carried
from the cardboard egg halves to the cereal bowls. The first team to finish
wins, though both teams keep their own sweets.

Musical Torch (Hallowe'en)

Number: any number   *Age:* 5–9   *Time:* no more than 5 minutes
Adult supervision: controlling music   (*Equipment:* source
of music, torch)

This is a game for playing after dark, so it's ideal for winter parties and is
a must for Hallowe'en parties with older children. Sit the players in a
circle and turn out the lights, so that the game begins in pitch darkness.
Turn on the torch and give it to the first player with the instruction to
hold it shining upwards just below the chin. This produces a frightening
eerie face! Start the music and let the players pass the torch from one to
another. The player holding the torch when the music stops has to drop
out. The last one left in is the winner. Players can make ghostly noises if
they like, to add to the effect of the game. You could play some suitably
eerie music too.

Apple Ducking (Hallowe'en) *

Number: any number   *Age:* any range (best for 5 upwards)
Time: 10 minutes or longer   *Adult supervision:* judging that no
hands are used and deciding on winner   (*Equipment:* a large
bowl of water and as many apples as there are players. Bibs,
towels and newspaper are also advisable, or waterproof
sheeting)

This traditional Hallowe'en game is not for those who worry about
undue mess. Any game involving children and water is likely to result in
wet floors and damp clothes, so be prepared. It's probably best played on
a washable floor, like the kitchen (though this might not be convenient if
a party tea is being prepared in there). If played on other surfaces, put
down a waterproof sheet, towels and newspapers.

You will need the largest bowl you can find (your washing-up bowl
if you can spare it). If there are more than six children playing, you may
need two or more bowls. Fill these with water and set some apples
bobbing in them. Provide your players with bibs or towels to protect
their clothes before play begins.

The players kneel round the bowl with their hands behind their
backs, and on the word 'Go!' they try and lift an apple from the bowl
using only their mouths and teeth. The first to do this is the winner.

Jingle Bells (Christmas)

Number: any number   *Age:* 6 upwards   *Time:* 3–5 minutes
Adult supervision: seeing that none of the blindfolded players
comes to harm   (*Equipment:* a bell, blindfolds for all but one of
the players)

Jingle Bells is a variation on another very popular game frequently
played at Christmas, *Blind Man's Buff.* In *Jingle Bells* all of the players
but one are blindfolded, and the odd one out is equipped with a bell. The
blindfolded players try to catch the player with the bell, guided towards
him by the sound alone. The first player to catch the one with the bell
changes places and the bellman dons the blindfold. (The player with the
bell is not allowed to hold the bell's clapper to prevent it from ringing –
that would be cheating.)

Merry Christmas *

Number: any number   *Age:* 7 upwards   *Time:* 3–5 minutes
Adult supervision: only to explain rules

The players form a circle holding hands at the start of this Christmas game. One player starts the game by counting 'One'. The player to the left follows with 'Two', and so on round the group, except that whenever the number 5 or any of its multiples come up, the player whose turn it is must not say the number; he has to say 'Merry Christmas' instead.

Any player who forgets to say 'Merry Christmas' in the right place, or says it in the wrong place, or says something like 'Happy Christmas' by mistake, leaves the group. The last player left counting is the winner.

Christmas Stocking Story

Number: any number   *Age:* 4 upwards   *Time:* 3–5 minutes
Adult supervision: making up and telling stories

This is a Christmas game that will appeal to very young players, although it does call on the imaginative powers of the adult giving the party.

Sit the players on the ground and give them their 'parts'. One will have his or her own name, the others will all be toys that might be put in the child's stocking: a teddy bear, a toy soldier, a doll, a colouring book – one object for each of the other children.

When they all know what each of them represents, the adult telling the story begins. Every time the child's name is mentioned, he or she must get up and turn around once before sitting down again. Every time one of the objects in the stocking is mentioned that player must get up and turn round in the same way. And every time the adult says 'Stocking', all the players get up and turn round before sitting down.

The story and the game ends with the words 'And the stocking was empty'. If there is a call for a second round, give each of the players a new identity.

Christmas Card Hunt *

Number: any number *Age:* 7 upwards *Time:* 5–10 minutes
Adult supervision: preparing old Christmas cards and judging
that they are properly matched up (*Equipment:* old Christmas
cards and a pair of scissors)

If you have ever wondered how to use up old Christmas cards, you might
consider turning them into this interesting and highly topical Christmas
game for children. Simply cut the cards in half, placing one half in a
large basket and the other in a pile to be scattered round the room.

Each player starts by taking one piece of a card from the basket and
then has to try and match this with the other half lying somewhere in the
room. Once the two halves of a card have been matched, the player is
allowed to take a second piece of card from the basket to try and match
that with its mate. At the end of the game the player with the most
matched cards is the winner.

SICKBED GAMES

Concentration *

Number: any number from 1 upwards *Age:* 8 upwards *Time:*
10–15 minutes *Adult supervision:* none (*Equipment:* page
from a magazine with lots of words and pictures, paper and
pencil per player)

There may not appear to be many games you can play when you are ill in
bed, but it's surprising how busy and interested a sick child can be with
the range of games that can be played.

Concentration is a game that can be played as well by one player as
by several. All that is required is a page from a magazine packed with
information either in pictures or words. The players are allowed two
minutes to study the page before putting it out of sight. Then they must
list as many things as they can remember.

Once one player has had a go, the page is passed to another who
does the same, and so on round the group. The player with the longest
list wins. If only one player is involved, he can check the page after
completing the list to see how good his memory is. Practice over a few
days will soon produce improvements.

The Nation Game *

Number: any number   *Age:* 8 upwards   *Time:* 5 minutes or longer   *Adult supervision:* judging answers and possibly competing   (*Equipment:* paper and pencil per player)

The players in this game have five minutes or longer in which to list as many 'nations' as they can think of. But these are nations with a difference. For once they are not the countries of the world like the USA, Sri Lanka and Australia – they are words that include the six letters in 'nation', words like 'donation', and 'imagination', 'examination', 'hibernation', etc. The player with the longest list at the end of the set time wins.

Word Links *

Number: 2   *Age:* 7 upwards   *Time:* 3–5 minutes
Adult supervision: none, except to take part possibly

The game begins with the players selecting a general topic from which they can easily think of different examples: names of countries, animals, flowers, trees, etc. The first player names one example from this group, and the second replies with another that begins with the last letter of the first example. Then the first player gives another example that begins with the last letter of the second example. The game continues with the players selecting words that form a continuous chain linked by first and last letters, until one player either uses a word that has already appeared in the chain, or is unable to think of a suitable word at all. When this happens the other player wins.

The Unicorn Game

Number: 1   *Age:* 6 upwards   *Time:* 10 minutes
Adult supervision: none

The Unicorn Game is one of the simplest, yet one of the most difficult, games to play. Try as hard as they like, it is almost impossible to succeed.

All a child has to do is lie in bed with his eyes shut for ten minutes. During those ten minutes he can think of anything he likes, anything under the sun, EXCEPT a unicorn. Strange as it may sound this is very hard to do. If in those six hundred seconds while he is lying there, a unicorn comes to mind, if only for a fraction of a second, then he has failed, though he shouldn't worry since most people do think of a unicorn at some time in that period, even when they don't mean to.

My House

Number: 1   *Age:* 6 upwards   *Time:* several hours over a number of days   *Adult supervision:* none except to provide material   (*Equipment:* scrap book, scissors, paste and a selection of old magazines and catalogues)

Children in bed for several days may well enjoy a project that will occupy them on and off throughout their illness and *My House* is one project that most children will enjoy working on.

A large scrap book becomes *My House*. In this the child uses a two-page spread to represent one room in the house and after laying out the ground-plan of rooms (and there can be as many as the 'owner' likes), the child becomes interior designer and starts decorating each room with cuttings of furniture, curtains and other features taken from a variety of magazines and catalogues.

As skill develops, the house may grow to include outbuildings and extra wings. If a form of 'temporary' pastings is used it will allow for changes of thought at a later stage – if a more suitable bathroom suite comes to light, for example.

The *My House* project may well last after the child has recovered, and in that case a second volume could well be called for.

Pyramids

Number: 1   *Age:* 8 upwards   *Time:* 10 minutes   *Adult supervision:* none   (*Equipment:* a pack of playing cards)

Here is another simple version of *Patience*, this time one that requires the cards to be laid down in the shape of a pyramid.

Play begins by removing the four aces from the pack. Shuffle the rest of the pack and deal the first twelve cards face downwards in the shape of a pyramid with one card at the top, two below it in the next row, three below them, and so on with two more rows of four and five cards respectively. The remaining cards form the stock. Once the pyramid is ready, two aces are placed face upwards on one side and the other two face upwards on the other side. The aim of the game is to place all the cards of the same suit in sequence on top of the correct ace, so all the hearts are piled on top of the ace of hearts, all the diamonds on top of the ace of diamonds, etc. The cards in the pyramid are turned up first, starting from the top, and every time one of these is transferred to one of the four piles, it is replaced by a card drawn from the stock. Cards that cannot be used in either an empty space or on a pile form a discard pile which can be drawn on when the original stock is exhausted.

The cards are only dealt once and if it hasn't been possible to complete the four suits using the cards from the pyramid as well as from the stock, the game has not worked out and the player must start once again and hope for better luck.

Where Am I? *

Number: 2 or more   *Age:* 6 upwards   *Time:* 2–3 minutes
Adult supervision: probably asking the 20 questions

This variation of *Twenty Questions* can be played by the child in bed and one visitor, or by the child and a group of others; in either case the rules are the same.

One player, usually the child in bed, thinks of a place and an activity he might be doing in the place, and asks, 'Where am I?' The other player, or players, now have twenty questions to try and discover where the player is and what he is doing. The only answers that can be given are 'Yes' and 'No', so it is up to the questioner to pick the most penetrating questions.

If the questioner hasn't guessed after the twentieth question, the player who asked 'Where am I?' can have another go.

Possible places and activities might be:

In the space shuttle flying to the moon.
At Wimbledon playing tennis.
At Lord's playing cricket.
Outside Buckingham Palace watching the changing of the
  Guard.

The Shortest Word *

Number: 2 or more   *Age:* 8 upwards   *Time:* 10 minutes or more   *Adult supervision:* providing list of letters and probably taking part   (*Equipment:* paper and pencil per player)

This is a quiet game for children well on the way to recovery who might enjoy a little challenging mental stimulus. Give the player or players a sheet of paper and pencil, and then list ten pairs of letters like these for example:

AG
AT
IP
ND
OP
PE
RT
SK
YO
ZO

Allow the players at least ten minutes in which to construct the shortest words they can, using one pair of letters in each word. With the above pairs you might get two sets of answers that look like this:

BAG	AGE
HAT	RAT
SLIP	PIP
OPEN	HOP
PEAR	PEA
PORT	ART
SKY	ASK
YOU	YOLK
ZONE	ZOO

The player with shortest words overall is the one with the list on the right and is the winner.

Name Messages

Number: 1   *Age:* 7 upwards   *Time:* 1 minute for every letter in the player's first name   *Adult supervision:* none   (*Equipment:* paper and pencil)

The player writes a first name (preferably his own) down the left-hand side of the sheet of paper and then writes it in reverse down the right-hand side. In the case of my own first name, my paper would look like this:

G	S
Y	E
L	L
E	Y
S	G

There are five letters in GYLES so I have five minutes to send messages to myself. I can send any message I like providing that it starts and ends with the two letters at either side of my page. So, after five minutes I might produce messages like these:

> Go to the shopS
> You should use a hankie when you sneezE
> Look at that huge hilL
> Ever felt hungrY?
> So I'm as snug as a bug in a ruG

The sentences don't have to be joined to one another and they can be made as funny as possible. The important point is that they should fit in between the letters in the name.

Clock Cards

Number: 1   *Age:* 8 upwards   *Time:* 10 minutes   *Adult supervision:* none   (*Equipment:* a pack of playing cards)

Shuffle the cards and deal them one at a time face down in the shape of an imaginary clock, so that a pile builds up on each of the hours and one in the centre at the point where the hands meet. When the dealing is finished there should be thirteen piles, each containing four cards.

The object of the game is to move the cards of the same value to the hours of the same value. So all the 2's should be moved to 2 o'clock, all the 7's to 7 o'clock and so on. It is the kings who occupy the spot in the centre.

The movement of the cards takes place like this. The top card of the pile in the centre is turned up and is tucked under the pile at its correct place on the clock-face, face upwards. If a queen was turned up, for example, she would be tucked under the four cards at 12 o'clock. The top card on the pile just added to is then turned up and the procedure follows as before.

You win by placing all the cards in the correct position before the four kings arrive in the centre. If the kings beat you to it, you lose.

Siege *

Number: 2   *Age:* 6 upwards   *Time:* 3–5 minutes
Adult supervision: only to draw playing area (if necessary)
(*Equipment:* paper and pencil, 4 counters)

This simple board game is well-suited for playing in bed. All that is needed is a drawing of a large rectangle with the corners joined by two diagonal lines. Each player has two counters (different colours per player). There are five places for the counters to go on the playing area, at the four corners and at the point in the centre where the diagonals cross. The players first take it in turns to place their counters, one at a time, on any of the five points. Players may move their counters along the lines from one point to another, provided the point moved to is vacant. When the four counters are on the board the aim of the game is to block the other player so that he is unable to move either counter. The player who does this wins the game.

Bright or Cloudy *

Number: 2   *Age:* 7 upwards   *Time:* 10 minutes   *Adult supervision:* none except to provide materials and possibly play as well   (*Equipment:* sheet from large calendar showing days of a 30-day month, a pack of cards, one black crayon, and one red crayon)

Bright or Cloudy is a weather game in which the players take it in turns to mark the days of the month on the calendar either red for Bright or black for Cloudy.

Before play begins, one player tosses a coin and the other calls 'heads' or 'tails'. The winner can decide to be either Bright or Cloudy. The cards are shuffled well and are placed face down in a pile.

Bright takes the top card to start play. If he draws a red card, he initials the first day of the month with the red pen. But if a black card is drawn, it must be discarded because players can only mark squares after drawing cards of their own colour. Now they take it in turns to draw and play cards until the month is filled with red or black marks. The player with the most days is the winner. If the cards are finished before the month is completed, reshuffle the pack and continue as before.

INDEX

Achi 48
Across the Great Divide 76
Acting Clumps 147
Acting Proverbs 149
Act the Word 143
Age Telling 161–2
A-Hunting We Will Go 6–7
Alphabet Angling 80
Alphabetical Sentences 170
Alphabet Race, The 2
Alquerque 60-1
American Hopscotch 88–9
Animal, Vegetable or Mineral 23
Ankle Race 129
Apple Ducking 196
A to Z 179
A Was an Apple Pie 20

Back to Front Race 127
Backward Spelling 135
Balloon Buffetting 18
Balloon Sweeping 128–9
Balloon Tennis 96
Ball Trap 93
Battleships 29–30
Beach Golf 184
Beach Olympics 189
Beetle 64–5
Beggar My Neighbour 44–5
Bingo 75
Birds Fly 3
Blindfold Drawing 157

Blind Hughie 71–2
Blind Man's Buff 111–12
Blind Man's Treasure
    Hunt 113–14
Blocking 71
Boiler Burst, The 179
Book Spotting 85–6
Bounce Eye 63
Boxes 30–1
Break Out 13
Bright or Cloudy 205
Build Up 174–5
Buried Words 81–2
Burst the Bag Race 132–3
Busy Bees 9
Button Bag 75

Capital Catching 24
Card Targets 14
Cat and Mouse 109
Catch and Pull 191
Charades 142–3
Cheat 41
Chess 51–4
Chicago 68
Choo-Choo Tag 11
Christmas Card Hunt 198
Christmas Stocking Story 197
Clear the Mark Leap-Frog 100
Clock Cards 203–4
Coffee Pot 19
Colour Changes 82

Colour Contest 177
Colour Dip 77
Concentration 198
Consequences 155–6
Consequences, Picture 35
Consonant Catalogue 22
Constantinople 153
Conversations 84
Corko 178–9
Crab Scuttle Relay 96
Crossing Out Letters 180

Daylight Robbery 9
Destination Please? 148
Dice Shot 64
Disappearing Coin 164
Dog and the Cat, The 84
Doll Dressing Race 132
Donkey (card game) 40
Donkey (talking game) 137
Donkey's Tail, The 114
Don't Stop Talking 139
Dotty Drawings 151
Dragon Heads and Tails 17–18
Draughts 57–8
Draughts-Board Observation 81
Dressing-up Race 133
Drop the Lot 128
Dumb Crambo 144–5
Dumb Nursery Rhymes 145–6
Dumb Show 144

Easter Bunnies and Chicks 194
Easter Egg Relay 195
Egg Guessing 194
Eh, Bee, Sea 183–4
Ends 70

Famous Fives 21
Farmer's in His Den, The 5–6
Farmyard 110

Feather Race 131
Feeder 95
Feel It 158
Fifty 68
Find the Adjectives 154
Fire! Fire! 17
First Names First 33
Fish 176–7
Fish Pond 107–8
Fish Pool 131–2
Fizz-Buzz 12
Flap Ears 11
Floating Feather, The 108
Follow My Leader 80
Fours 70 1
Fox and Geese 61–2
French Cricket 187
French Hop (Snail) 90
Four Field Kono 49–50

Game of Shadows, The 164
Geography 171
Giant's Steps 15
Gobang 50
Go Boom 44
Gora 15
Grand Chain 123
Grandmother's Footsteps 113
Grand Old Duke of York,
  The 121–2
Grasshopper 55–6
Guess in the Dark 32

Handkerchief 97–8
Hand Puppets 159–60
Hangman 28–9
Happy Families 39–40
Heads and Tails 152
Hearts 66
Heart Throbs 193
Heights 83

Here We Come Gathering Nuts in May 10
Here We Go Round the Mulberry Bush 122–3
Hic, Haec, Hoc 168
Hide and Seek 74
Hole in the Sheet 193
Hopping Home 94
Hop Rabbit Hop 111
Hopscotch 185–6
Hopscotch, American 88–9
Hop, Step and Jump 99
Horseshoe 55
Hot Boiled Beans and Bacon 3
Huntsman and the Hares 91
Hunt the Alphabet 87
Hunt the Thimble 112

I Love My Love 21
Initial I-Spy 108
I Packed My Bag 134
Islands 177–8
I Spy 138
I Want a Rhyme 141–2

Jack, Jack, the Bread Burns 91
Jingle Bells 196
Join the Numbers 32
Jolly Miller 101
Jousting 16
Judge, The 135
Jumbled Proverbs 152
Just a Minute 87

Kangaroo Racing 97
Kayles 69
Kim's Game 150–1
King Caesar 88
King Canute's Game 188
King of the Castle 14–15

Lemon Relay 13
Letter Sentence 156
Lifting the Ice Cube 161
London Bridge 124

Madelinette 56–7
Magic Discs 160
Marbles Race 129
Merry Christmas 197
Middle Man 187
Mile's End 173
Mind Reading 79
Minister's Cat, The 139
Minute Words 20
Mirror Images 31
Missing Vowels 158
Mora 169
Musical Arches 116
Musical Bumps 117
Musical Chairs 120
Musical Hats 125
Musical Hotch-Potch 117
Musical Islands 119
Musical Numbers 125
Musical Posture 123
Musical Reflexes 119–20
Musical Slipper 124–5
Musical Statues 121
Musical Torch 195
Musical Walking Stick 120–1
Mu-Torere 58–9
My House 200
My Ship Sails 43

Name Chain 76
Name Messages 203
Nation Game, The 199
News Line 31
Newspaper Quiz 182
Nim 69–70
Nine Holes 49

Nine Men's Morris 47–8
Noah's Ark 146
North, South, East and West 92
Number-Plate Messages 171–2
Number-Plate Numbers 170

Observation 175
Obstacle Courses 79
Old Maid 38
Old Oak Chest, The 138
Oranges and Lemons 118–19

Pairing Up 36
Pall Mall 98
Parties 104–7
  Food and Drink 106
  On the Day 106–7
  Planning 104–6
Pat-a-Cake 7–8
Paul Jones 116–17
Pavement Bullboard 178–80
Pelmanism 36–7
Pennies in the Circle 110
Penny Dropping 5
Pick and Cup Race 130
Picture Consequences 35
Picture Spotting 156–7
Pig 66–7
Pin Weed 185
Please Pass 150
Poison Letters 136
Poor Pussy 148–9
Potato Race 128
Pyramids 200–1

Queenie 178

Rattle Catcher 14
Reversi 59–60
Rhyme Counting 26
Ring Taw 63

Rolling Stone 42
Romeo and Juliet 192
Roundabout Escape 18
Rounders 98–9
Round the Clock 67
Round the Corner 42–3
Round-the-World Relay 86
Rummy 46–7

Sausages 141
Scrambles 87–8
Secrets 134
Sentences 24–5
Sevens 92
Shadow Shows 165
Shebble Game, The 191
Ship Game 83
Shoot 169
Shopping 78
Shortest Word, The 202
Siege 204
Simon Says 145
Sing a Song of Sixpence 4
Sir Tommy 172
Skimmers 190
Slap Jack 181
Smell It Out 35
Snail, or French Hop 90
Snail's Race 130–1
Snap 37–8
Snip 27
Snip-Snap-Snorem 39
Snow Snake 181
Socky Ball 2
Sounds Off 153
Spangy 62
Spelling Bee 24
Spinning the Plate 115–16
Spoof 173
Spot the Number 78
Square Chasing 100

Squaring Up 33–4
Squat Tag 182–3
Squeak, Piggy, Squeak 109
Squirts 192
Stretch and Bend 16–17
Synonyms 82

Tag 93–4
Teacher 77
Tennis, Elbow, Foot 26
Ten Pennies 155
Thimble Race 126
Three Against One 190
Three Blind Mice 8
Tongue Twisters 163
Touch Tag 183
Touch Wood and Whistle 90
Tourist Trail 22
Traffic Lights 74
Travellers Tales 25
Triangular Tug of War 182
Twenty Questions 140
Twigs 188

Unicorn Game, The 199–200

Up and Over Down and Under 16

Waiter! Waiter! 126
War 45
Water Relay 186
Whack and Catch 96–7
What Are We? 147–8
What Are We Shouting? 135–6
What's Changed 84
What's My Name? 140
Where Am I? 201
White Spot, The 93
Who Am I? 23
Who Leads? 12
Whoop 95
Winking 115
Word Chains 19–20
Word Links 199
Word Power 154
Word Watching 174
Word Wise 27
Worm, The 34

Zoo Twins 7
ZYX 28